¡PASAPO

READING STRATEGIES IN SPANISH

Kathleen Moore, EdD
Edward Baranowski, PhD

California State University

KENDALL/HUNT PUBLISHING COMPANY
4050 Westmark Drive Dubuque, Iowa 52002

ISBN 0-7575-1164-3

Printed in the United States of America
10 9 8 7 6 5 4 3 2 1

DEDICATION

The authors wish to dedicate
Pasaporte a la lectura
to all students of the
Spanish language.
May their study of reading strategies
lead them to a greater understanding of
the language and culture of the
Hispanic world.

TABLE OF CONTENTS

PREFACE

This textbook is unique in that it focuses on only one language skill: reading.

While most language courses are driven by the four language skill areas of listening, speaking, reading and writing, this text has been written to facilitate student learning so that, at the conclusion of the course, the student will have mastered the strategies necessary to read a variety of authentic cultural materials in Spanish with a high degree of competence.

It is recommended that you use English as the vehicle for most of the instruction. The students will study the specific reading strategies and apply their learning in a variety of activities. Again, the goal of this course is not communicative competence. There will be opportunities to use the target language to expose the students to the spoken language, but the authors caution you not to require this of the students. Another suggestion is to avoid lengthy grammatical explanations. The goal of this course is to apply the reading strategies outlined in the text and become proficient in reading. The authors also encourage the use of other authentic reading materials that you deem challenging and supportive of this goal.

Do keep in mind the student outcomes/objectives of Spanish 7. At the completion of this course, students will be able to:

- demonstrate pre-reading skills by identifying topic and organization of authentic material
- use pre-reading strategies and identify probable content
- skim for information
- decode for main ideas and, with skill-building activities, decode for details
- decode cross-references and metaphor
- demonstrate comprehension of point-of-view, tone of material
- write brief summaries of reading passages
- respond to context and content
- recognize basic grammatical structures and use this knowledge to decode authentic material

- demonstrate knowledge of the 5Cs of the National Standards – Communities, Connections, Cultures, Comparisons, and Communication

The authors also encourage the use of authentic web sites to offer students more practice in reading a variety of texts in Spanish. Use the Appendices at the end of the text to support your instructional strategies and refer to Appendix B early on in the course so as to familiarize students with the techniques for using their bilingual dictionary correctly. Appendix A is intended to be a quick at-a-glance summary of major points of grammar for student reference.

ACKNOWLEDGMENTS

The authors would like to thank their friends and colleagues for their support and encouragement in the publication of this textbook. It is their hope that all who use the text will be inspired to continue their language study and enjoy the challenges of reading authentic material in Spanish.

Special thanks to :

Doug Sapola, CSU Sacramento – Technical Support
Kena Warrick, Sutter Middle School – Technical Support
Eve Brazney, Sutter Middle School – Artwork

NOTE TO THE STUDENT

As you begin this course, you may think that reading authentic texts in Spanish is a daunting task. At the conclusion of your study, you will be amazed at just how much you will be able to read and understand, simply by employing the reading strategies that you will practice. Remember that reading is a process of specific steps. You must be actively engaged in this process, recognizing that you bring a good deal of background knowledge and daily experience to the process. Reading also involves context and connections and does not require that you understand every word. Further, it is a mental activity which requires concentration and application of previous knowledge for greater understanding. By the end of this course, you will be able to:

- demonstrate pre-reading skills by identifying topic and organization of authentic material
- use pre-reading strategies and identify probable content
- decode for main ideas and, with skill-building activities, decode for details
- decode cross-references and metaphor
- write brief summaries of reading passages
- respond to context and content
- recognize basic grammatical structures and use this knowledge to decode authentic material
- demonstrate knowledge of the 5Cs of the National Standards – Communities, Connections, Cultures, Comparisons, Communications

Another reference text to support your study is your faithful dictionary; remember to bring it with you to class. You will learn how to use a dictionary correctly in the course of your study as there is a very fine dictionary section in Appendix B. Appendix A provides you with a quick at-a-glance summary of major grammatical points.

Enjoy your study of the reading strategies. ¡Adelante!

Professor Kathleen Moore   Professor Edward Baranowski

PRE-READING STRATEGIES
Introduction

As you begin your study of reading strategies in Spanish, it is important to realize that you use the very same techniques when reading in your own language. (Language One) You may even discover that you will enhance your reading skills in your native language by studying and applying the skills you will learn in this course. The objective here is to give you the basic tools necessary to be able to read with a high degree of comprehension authentic materials written in Spanish.

Remember that reading is a **PROCESS,** a mental activity that involves **READING** within a **CONTEXT.** It is an **ACTIVE** and **INTERACTIVE** process: the writer communicates ideas to the reader and the reader expects to understand them. We often read for pure pleasure or to seek information about a topic. Thus, we will read in a cursory manner, to get the gist, or we will read for detailed information, also known as close reading. Whatever the intent, the following pre-reading strategies will help you to read authentic materials in Spanish.

Lesson 1

FORMAT

The first step in the reading process is to recognize the **FORMAT** of the text. The format will provide many clues to aid you in the interpretation of the text. First, **SCAN** the entire passage. How is it organized? What is it in the reading material that is **FAMILIAR** to you? How is it organized? What is it in the passage that is already familiar to you? What do the **TITLE, SUBTITLES** and the words in **BOLD PRINT** suggest to you?

Also, there is a universal technique that is used to interpret and understand any text. The reader should always ask the questions: **Who? What? Where? When? Why? How?** Use these questioning techniques whenever you approach a text – in any language! You will notice that many of the questions in this text use these useful interrogative words.

Activity A. Look at the texts below and choose the number that best describes them.

A.

¡Consigue tu
taza de café
GRATIS
con este
cupón!

1. An ad
2. An announcement
3. A coupon

B.

Descubra
MEXICO..
¡Viaje con
AVIANCA
HOY!

1. An ad
2. An announcement
3. A coupon

C.

El 6 de enero, 2003

Querido Mario,
¿Cómo estás? ¿Qué hay de nuevo? Yo estoy bien pero sigo trabajando muchas horas y no me gusta. Escríbeme pronto.
Julia

1. A letter
2. A bibliography

You probably found this to be quite easy. That is because the format of the written text gives you many clues as to what it is about. With your **background knowledge**, you already know what to expect in such formats.

Now answer the following questions.

1. In A, what is it that one can get?

2. How much does the item cost?

3. What does one need to present to get the item offered?

4. In B, what country can one visit?

5. What airline is offering its travel services?

6. To whom is Julia writing?

7. What is the date?

8. What does Julia want Mario to do?

Even with these few examples, you see that it is not so difficult to identify texts and interpret the message.

Activity B. Now, look at the following texts and see if you can guess what they refer to. Be sure to focus on the format features such as illustrations, photos, graphs, graphics, charts, etc.

A.

DON PABLO ESNAL GUILLAR
Actor

Falleció en Jilotepec, México
El día 15 de octubre de 2002

D.E.P.

Toda la familia ruega le recuerden en sus oraciones y se unan a las intenciones de las misas que se celebrarán por su alma en México D.F.

1. A weather report 2. An obituary 3. A boarding pass

Now answer the following questions.

1. The announcement concerns whom?
2. What happened?
3. When did this take place?
4. Where did this take place?
5. Who is requesting prayers for this person?
6. Where will the Masses be celebrated?
7. What was the profession of Don Pablo?
8. What do you think **D.E.P.** means?

Using these format clues and your background knowledge, you can read and understand more than you think!

Activity C. Identify this text.

Carmen Torres **ANTOLOGIA DE POESIA MODERNA BOLIVIANA** Editorial Siquieros San Juan, Puerto Rico 2002

1. TV Guide   2. Book title   3. Newspaper ad

Now answer the following questions.

1. What is the title?
2. What type of publication is this?
3. When was this published?
4. Who is the author?
5. Who published this work?
6. What is the topic?
7. Where was this published?

The term **background knowledge** was mentioned above. There is much that we all have in common even though we do not speak the same language. There is what we could term an international familiarity with experiences and things that we share in common. Just think of the format clues of the advertising world. It is not hard to discover that such texts are written to attract the buyer and entice him/her to buy the product. What the reader brings to the text is a variety of experiences, interests and knowledge about the world. **Context,** combined with this background knowledge, enables the reader to understand a great deal without having to resort to dictionary searches and grammar books.

The following activities will give you some more practice with identifying format clues in order to understand the text that you are reading.

Activity D. Identify this text.

¡ATENCION, INQUILINOS!
¿Por qué pagar renta ?
¡ Ud. puede ser

¡PROPIETARIO
de su propia
CASA!

Consulte López Financial. Podemos ayudarle a encontrar y financiar

la casa de sus sueños...

Nos especializamos en:

- Compras con 3% enganche
- ¿Mal crédito? ¡No hay problema!
- Refinanciamientos

¡Llame hoy mismo! 1-800-534-5341

¡Estamos Para Servir A Nuestra Comunidad!

1. A receipt 2. An ad 3. A promotion with a coupon

Now answer the following questions.

1. What is this text about?

2. What is the name of the company?

3. What does this company promise?

4. What does this company specialize in?

5. Who might be interested in their services?

6. What do you think *enganche* means?

7. How can a prospective client contact this company?

8. What do you think this phrase means: *"¡Estamos Para Servir A Nuestra Comunidad!"*

The **titles**, **subtitles** and **layout** of the text give many clues as to the topic and content of the text. These are often printed in bold type. Study the following texts:

A.

Para Viajeros

España	M.	m.
Algeciras	22	10
Alicante	31	25
Barcelona	29	23
Burgos	30	17
Córdoba	30	16
Granada	32	17
León	27	17
Murcia	35	23
Palma	33	20
Segovia	27	17
Toledo	30	20

Abreviaturas:
M = Temperatura máxima
m = Temperatura mínima centígrado

B.

AVIACO
AEROLINEA
PERUANA
Su número de asiento
2A
Sin fumar

PASE DE ABORDAR

Por favor, verifique su número de asiento y guarde este pase.

¡BIENVENIDO A BORDO!

C.

S. Francisco Salas Muñoz
y
María Angelina Sinaloa de Salas

Oscar López Santos
y
Lucía Paulina Day de López

Participan el Enlace Matrimonial de sus hijos
Margarita María y Ramón
Y tienen el honor de invitarle a la ceremonia religiosa
que se celebrará en el Templo de Nuestra Señora del Carmen
El día 5 de noviembre de 2002 a la 1:00 p.m.

Cuernavaca, Morelos

Activity E. Identify the topics of A, B, C.

1. A

2. B

3. C

Now answer the following questions.

1. In text A, what meaning can you get from *Viajeros*? (Hint: v*iajar* means to travel)

2. This text is in reference to what country?

3. What do the numbers refer to?

4. What does M mean? m?

5. What do you know about the weather in Toledo?

6. In text B, when would you use this?

7. What does *Sin fumar* mean?

8. What is the date of the event and what is going to take place?

9. Where will this event take place?

10. Who is announcing this event?

11. What are Margarita and Ramón going to do?

Again, as you begin the reading process, look for format features such as titles, typefaces, captions, size of type and kind (italics, etc.), illustrations, and layout. These will give you clues as to the context and specific content.

Activity F. Now look at the following texts and identify the format features.

A.

ATENCION JOVENES

Si tienen más de 18 años y están interesados en trabajar para nuestra compañía,

LLAMEN AHORA
O MANDENNOS ESTA INFORMACION

Nombre__________________
Domicilio__________________
Teléfono__________________

COPIMUNDO
Vicente #3 Guadalajara
TEL. 0452-435

B.

LEO

(JULIO23/AGOSTO 22)

Las relaciones con sus asociados y con sus amigos ocuparán su mente hasta el 16. A partir del 21, Júpiter favorecerá las actividades financieras. Tenga cuidado con lo que hace con su dinero antes del día 21. Después, aproveche para firmar contratos y resolver problemas personales. La luna llena indica suerte para Ud.

1. Title__________________ __________________
2. Subtitles__________________ __________________
3. Illustrations__________________ __________________
4. Type changes__________________ __________________

Now answer these questions.

1. In text A, what is being offered?

2. To whom is this being offered?

3. What is the name of the company? What type of work does the company do?

4. What is text B about and where would you find this type of text?

5. What does *la luna llena* promise for this person?

Activity G: More practice with format! Circle the number that best describes the two texts below.

A.

LA HOJA VERDE
¡Que disfruten!

¡Platos vegetarianos para todos los gustos!

Se abre lunes a sábado 12 a 20
Santa Ana #43 1er. Piso
TEL 54-9798

1. A receipt
2. An article from a newspaper
3. An ad

B.

METRO
329-5
Sencillo

Utilización
según
tarifas

68594

1. A ticket
2. A receipt
3. An ad

Now answer the following questions.

1. In text B, where would you likely get this?
2. What do you think *sencillo* means in this context?
3. What kind of a place is indicated in text A?
4. What could you expect to get there?
5. When is this place open?
6. Is the telephone number listed? And the address?

Activity H: The following pictures belong to a context associated with:

a.

b.

c.

1. sports 2. weather 3. tourism 4. medicine

***El mundo hispano* connection.**

For more practice in format clues, look on pages 2, 3 and 4 of your text *El mundo hispano*. At the top of page 2, there are 3 symbols that give a clue as to what this text is about. Identify the 3 symbols. What do they have to do with the woman in the picture? What is her profession?

On page 3, you see another symbol that will immediately let you know what is being discussed. What does the title in bold refer to? The subtitle is in reference to what? What does the pie chart on the top right of the page indicate?

The title on page 4 indicates that there will be a discussion of the Hispanic world. What do we call the information moving horizontally by date? Your background knowledge and the context are clues to your understanding of the topic.

READING PURPOSE

The next step is to identify your **reading purpose**. What do you expect to find out? One of the most important factors to keep in mind when you read is the fact that you, as a reader, bring a depth of background knowledge to your reading task. For example, when reading a TV guide, you are already quite familiar with the format and the type of information that a guide of this kind offers—programming, dates, times and channels. If you were to look at a horoscope page, you would already know the type of information such a piece would offer you--zodiac signs, birthdays, predictions for the future, advice and so on.

Activity A. With this in mind, give 3 bits of information that you expect to find in the following:

a. commercial telephone listing

____

b. table of contents

____

c. business card

____

d. want ad

____

e. wedding announcement

____

f. obituary

____

g. coupon

____

h. menu

____

If you know what type of information you are looking for, you can easily adapt to unfamiliar ways of presenting familiar material. Whether in L1 or L2[1], you already have an idea of what you hope to learn by reading the piece and you can easily **GUESS!**

[1] L1 (Language 1) is the speakers primary language and L2 (Language 2) is the language being learned as a second language.

Lesson 2

SCANNING AND GUESSING FOR FURTHER ORGANIZATIONAL CLUES

So far you have discovered that you can gather much information through the scanning and guessing process. You also have been made aware of the fact that you bring to the reading process a tremendous amount of background knowledge to aid you in understanding what you are reading. Thus, you can comprehend a great deal without knowing much Spanish; it is not such a daunting task! As you have seen, the pre-reading strategies will continue to emphasize the importance of scanning the format. In the next level of study, you will learn to focus on familiar vocabulary within the body of the text.

THE COGNATE

A **cognate** is a word that is similar in both languages and is easily understood. There might be a slight change in spelling and, of course, the pronunciation will differ, but the cognate in context is easily recognizable. There are hundreds of cognates in Spanish that you can readily understand and interpret. Look at the following examples:

1. *el professor* - the professor
2. *la clase* - the class
3. *la pronunciación* - the pronunciation
4. *estudiar* - to study
5. *el animal* - the animal
6. *la nación* - the nation
7. *extrovertido* - extrovert
8. *especial* - special
9. *famoso* - famous
10. *el auto* - the auto, car

As you become more aware of the cognate, recognize that there are some constants. For example, words that end in "-tion" and "-sion" in English have Spanish cognates that end in *ción* and –*sión*; these are always feminine in gender. Here is a list of other endings that will help you identify cognates.

	Spanish[2]	English	Spanish[2]	English
❑	*-ción*	-tion	*acción*	action
❑	*-sión*	-sion	*tensión*	tension
❑	*-dad*	-ty	*ciudad*	city
❑	*-mento*	-ment	*departamento*	department (also, apartment)
❑	*-miento*	-ment	*movimiento*	movement

Note that there are no double consonants in Spanish except "cc" and, rarely, a double "n." The combinations "ll" and "rr" are considered to be separate letters that represent an individual sound.

Prefixes, found at the beginning of a word, are very helpful in identifying cognates as well. Here are a few examples:

	Spanish	English	Spanish[2]	English
❑	*pre-*	pre-	*prehistórico*	prehistoric
❑	*in-*	in-, un-	*incontrolable*	uncontrollable
❑	*des-*	de-	*destruir*	to destroy
❑	*re-*	re-	*reaccionar*	to react
❑	*pos-, post-*	post-	*posgraduado*	postgraduate
❑	*-ancia, -encia*	ance, ence	*evidencia, arrogancia*	evidence, arrogance

Some common **suffixes** (word endings) are:

❑	*-ble*	-ble	*operable*	operable
❑	*-ía*	-y; -ie	*teología, caloría*	theology, calorie
❑	*-ico*	-ic, -ical	*alcohólico, cómico*	alcoholic, comical
❑	*-ismo*	-ism, -ysm	*naturalismo*	naturalism
❑	*-ino, -ina*	-in, -ine	*penicilina, medicina*	penicillin, medicine

---

[2] Note the use of the written accent mark.

True cognates have exactly the same spelling and meaning in Spanish and English and thus are easily recognized and understood. Some of these words are: *evento, visible, color, animal, radio.*

Some very common words in Spanish lend themselves to other meanings in English. A few of these are: *terminar* "to finish," but also to terminate; *ambicioso* "ambitious," but not in a positive light (i.e., "over-ambitious").

Activity A: Look at these Spanish words and give the English meaning.

1. *auto*
2. *brillante*
3. *chileno*
4. *cultura*
5. *doctor*
6. *ejemplos*
7. *especialmente*
8. *estudiante*
9. *famoso*
10. *fútbol*
11. *generoso*
12. *historia*
13. *influencia*
14. *mural*
15. *notable*
16. *parte*
17. *simple*
18. *televisión*
19. *vanidad*
20. *zoológico*

Activity B. Match the English equivalents of these words.

1. *hostilidad*
2. *nación*
3. *creación*
4. *extensión*
5. *tranquilidad*
6. *imposible*
7. *familia*
8. *determinación*
9. *nacionalidad*
10. *supremacía*

a. determination
b. creator
c. nationality
d. nation
e. supremacy
f. family
g. extension
h. creation
i. impossible
j. tranquil
k. tranquility
l. extended
m. hostility
n. impossiblity
o. familial

FALSE COGNATES

Just when you thought it was safe to move about freely in the world of the cognate, it is necessary to bring up the issue of the false cognate or "false friend". There are words in Spanish that seem to be cognates but are not. Yet, how does one really know if it is a cognate or not? A good rule-of-thumb is that the word most likely is a cognate, but beware! If you have any doubts, look it up.

A classic example of a false friend is the word *embarazada*, which appears to mean "embarrassed". Unfortunately, the word really means "pregnant" (With this in mind, it could not be *embarazad**o***, right?) and has gotten a lot of people into trouble! There are others, as well. *Contestar* in English means to "answer," not to "contest" (*disputar*). Also, *una lectura* is not a "lecture" but a reading; *una conferencia* is a "lecture." Study the following list of *cognados falsos* and be aware of these as you practice your reading skills in Spanish.

SPANISH	**SPANISH SYNONYMS**	**ENGLISH**
1. *soportar*	*mantener, apoyar*	to tolerate (**not** to support)
2. *simpático*	*agradable, compasivo*	nice, congenial (**not** sympathetic)
3. *realizar*	*llevar a cabo, lograr*	*t*o accomplish (**not** to realize)
4. *los parientes*	*los familiares*	the relatives (**not** parents)
5. *relativo*	*en cuanto a*	relative to, about (**not** relative as in family member)
6. *gracioso*	*cómico*	funny, witty (**not** gracious)

SPANISH	SPANISH SYNONYMS	ENGLISH
7. *injuriar*	*insultar*	to insult (**not** to injure)
8. *ignorar*	*no saber*	to be unaware of (**not** to ignore)
9. *rudo*	*mal educado*	crass, uneducated (**not** rude)
10. *actual*	*en el momento, hoy en día*	present, these days (**not** actual, real)

Activity A. Define the following cognates.

1. la existencia _______________ *6. tráfico*_______________

2. imposible _________________ *7. directo*_______________

3. el valle ___________________ *8. influencia*_____________

*4. la exterminación*____________ *9. producto*_____________

5. *transparente*_______________ *10. final*_______________

Activity B. Write the Spanish cognate for the following English words.

1. action________________________ 6. description___________

2. ambition______________________ 7. election______________

3. attention______________________ 8. emotion______________

4. celebration___________________ 9. intention_____________

5. condition_____________________ 10. revolution___________

Activity C. Write the Spanish cognate for the following English words.

1. authority____________________ 6. nationality_____________
2. credibility__________________ 7. opportunity____________
3. felicity______________________ 8. negativity______________
4. maternity____________________ 9. necessity______________
5. personality__________________ 10. insincerity____________

Activity D. Write the Spanish cognate for the following English words.

1. document __________________ 6. department____________
2. element____________________ 7. sacrament____________
3. ligament____________________ 8. movement(ie)_________
4. sediment____________________ 9. sentiment(ie)_________
5. temperment ________________ 10. increment____________

Activity E. Look at the following ads and list the cognates that you find.

A.

COPITODO INTERNACIONAL

ENCARGUE SUS COPIAS
ESTARAN LISTAS DENTRO DE
24 HORAS

2,50 Pts. la fotocopia

Reducciones, Ampliaciones y Copias Especiales

Nota: Copias en el acto 3,00 Pts.

Teléfono: 410 33 23
#34 Plaza Mayor

1. ____________________ 6. ____________________

2. ____________________ 7. ____________________

3. ____________________ 8. ____________________

4. ____________________ 9. ____________________

5. ____________________ 10. ____________________

B.

BANCO DE CREDITO

¿Usted necesita $$?

¡No espere más!

Permítanos echarle la mano con lo que necesita para modernizar su casa, pagar sus deudas, disfrutar de unas vacaciones.

¡Tenemos un préstamo sobre el valor neto de su casa que también resultará en una ventaja sobre los impuestos!

Para saber cuánto dinero Ud. puede obtener prestado de su casa, simplemente llene los datos necesarios.

_____ Valor actual de la casa
_____ x 0.90
_____ (-) Su préstamo hipotecario
_____ = Total del valor neto financiable

Llame hoy mismo al (800) 555-5454

1. ____________________ 6. ____________________

2. ____________________ 7. ____________________

3. ____________________ 8. ____________________

4. ____________________ 9. ____________________

5. ____________________ 10. ____________________

Activity F. Scan the following passage looking for cognates. Make a list and then define them.

"¿Qué es una leyenda?"
Susana Aguirre Hernández

La mayoría de los pueblos indígenas mexicanos – los aztecas, mayas, tlaxcaltecas, zapotecas, etc.--utilizaban narraciones fantásticas o leyendas que contenían símbolos representativos de cada una de estas culturas. Contaban sus historias de generación en generación para que éstas no murieran. Las historias fueron contadas con cada vez más esmero para que todo el que perteneciera a ellas conociera su pasado, sus raíces y su origen, para descubrir adónde debía encaminar sus pasos.

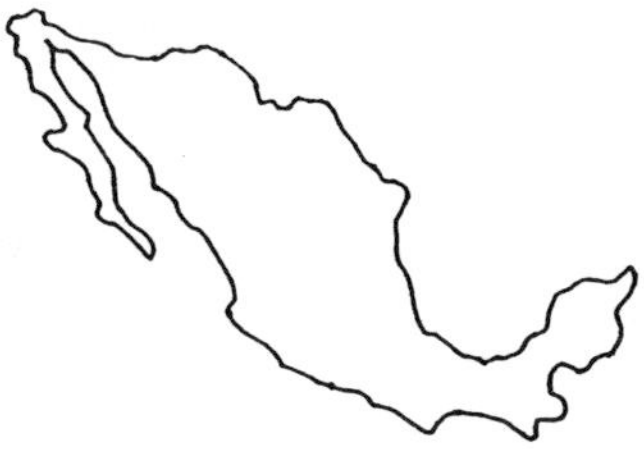

Activity G: Now read this passage, listing the cognates that you find. What is it about?

"Día de gran tradición en México"
Susana Aguirre Hernández

Las tradiciones son costumbres establecidas y heredadas por generaciones que se cumplen lo más fielmente posible desde un principio y así son continuadas por años y años.

México tiene la característica de ser un pueblo de tradiciones muy bien arraigadas y definidas. México, además de ser conocido como una nación alegre y festiva, cuenta con unas fiestas que siempre tendrán un sentido especial, un porqué. La mayoría de las ocasiones no sólo serán "profanas" o alejadas de las cuestiones sagradas, sino que, al contrario, estarán relacionadas con la religión católica, que es la que profesa la mayoría de sus habitantes.

Incluso algunas celebraciones combinan costumbres prehispánicas con las que se establecieron a partir de la colonia, o sólo adaptan los cultos de dioses prehispánicos a la nueva doctrina cristiana-católica. Por eso, es común encontrar correspondencias en fechas y formas de representar algunos hechos y, al conmemorarlos, no sólo se participa en la fiesta religiosa sino que también se conoce un poco de historia.

Recognizing Familiar Borrowed Words and Cognates

Sometimes when you are reading an article in a newspaper or a menu at a restaurant or a passage of historical or political significance, you will find some words that have been borrowed from a foreign language.

Activity A. What language do you associate with the following words?

1. ____	soupe du jour	7. ________	ballet
2. ____	pizza	8. ________	salsa
3. ____	rodeo	9. ________	kraut
4. ____	burritos	10. ________	lasagna
5. ____	tango	11. ________	coup d'état
6. ____	alcohol	12. ________	restaurant

a. Arabic b. Italian c. Spanish d. French
e. German

You have learned that **cognates** are similar in form and meaning in the L1 and L2. These words are an important source of information which helps you to understand the main ideas within the text. But be careful! Again, be aware of those **false cognates.** In the preceding activities, you worked with real cognates. Now, look at these words to determine if there are false cognates or true cognates.

Activity B. From the list below, circle C if the word is a cognate and FC if it is a false cognate. Then write the equivalent in English.

1. *nacionalidad* C FC =________________
2. *asistir* C FC =_________________
3. *televisión* C FC=________________
4. *actualmente* C FC=________________
5. *sopa* C FC=________________
6. *atender* C FC=________________

Finding out the "who", "what", "when", "where", "why", "how", in the reading passage.

Another reading strategy that is most effective is seeking to discover the "who", "what", "when", "where", "why", "how". Asking these leading questions will help you to pinpoint and isolate critical information related to the main idea of the passage. With this in mind, see if you can answer these questions after reading the passage.

"No llores por mí, Argentina"

Una de las personas más controversiales en la historia argentina fue Eva Perón o "Evita", el nombre especial que le dieron los argentinos. Esta ex-actriz se enamoró del presidente de aquel entonces, Juan Perón, pero fue rechazada por la alta sociedad a causa de su vida escandalosa y sus orígenes muy humildes. Evita siempre quería ayudar a su gente y se dedicó a muchas causes sociales con el fin de avanzar los derechos humanos de sus paisanos. Le causaba mucho dolor ver la miseria y la injusticia que se encontraban en su país. Para muchos argentinos, Evita Perón es una santa aunque sigue siendo la causa de mucha controversia en la Argentina.

Activity A. Answer the following questions based on the passage that you just read.

1. Who is this passage about?
2. Where was she from?
3. What did she do in her life?
4. How did she come to be so involved in the affairs of her country?
5. Why was Evita rejected by many of her countrymen?
6. When did she begin most of her work for human rights?

Activity B. Scan the following passage and see if you can answer the questions that follow.

¿Qué se recomienda para una buena alimentación?

Muchísimos nutriólogos, como la Dra. Carmen Jiménez Gil, recomiendan una dieta bien balanceada para gozar de buena salud. Según ellos, es importante ingerir pocos alimentos de origen animal (carne, huevos, etc.) en la dieta del adulto. Deben consumirlos principalmente los niños y los adolescentes, puesto que están en pleno desarrollo.

Es necesario incluir en sus comidas frutas y verduras, ya que son de una vital importancia para el organismo. Las verduras de color verde son especialmente importantes en la dieta diaria. Es importante consumir pocas grasas y azúcares. Es mejor consumir cereales como el arroz integral, el trigo y el maíz. Además de ser deliciosos, son muy nutritivos. También, hay que consumir tubérculos como la papa y el camote y las leguminosas como el frijol, las alubias y las lentejas.

Finalmente, los nutriólogos recomiendan que se evite la sal en exceso, el tabaco, el alcohol y los alimentos procesados y con conservantes.

Use these questions as a guide when doing your close reading.

1. Who is speaking? Who is the article about? Who are the key people mentioned?

2. What is the main idea? What information can you get from this passage?

3. Where is the event, action, process taking place?

4. When is the event, action, process taking place?

5. Why is this person, event, action, process important? Significant?

6. How does the person, event, action, process affect us?

Activity C. Now read the following and ask the same questions as above.

Días de celebración

Susana Aguirre Hernández

La Navidad es un ejemplo de una celebración enorme en casi todos los países del mundo. En México, es un día religioso muy importante y es el primero en una serie de otros días festivos que incorporan muchas celebraciones importantes. Claro, las

Posadas inician estos días festivos el día dieciséis de diciembre, terminando con la Navidad. Luego, hay la fiesta de los Santos Inocentes, el 28 de diciembre, día en que se recuerda la persecución del Rey Herodes a los niños menores de tres años para matar al recién nacido Jesús. El 6 de enero se celebra la llegada de los Santos Reyes Magos a Belén. En este día, los niños mexicanos reciben sus regalitos de los tres Reyes Magos. El Día de la Candelaria, el 2 de febrero, representa la Purificación de María en el templo y la presentación del Niño Jesús. Con esta fiesta, se cierra el ciclo de estas fiestas importantes.

Lesson 3

SKIMMING FOR INFORMATION

This is another pre-reading technique that will aid you in pinpointing more detailed information in longer and more challenging reading passages. What you do is to let your eyes move methodically but quickly over the written material, trying to focus on a particular word, phrase, sentence or detail. In the skimming process, you are constantly asking the key questions of **who, what, when, where, why** and **how** in the passage while keying in on the format cues.

Skimming is very helpful in the reading process because it combines elements of the scanning techniques that you have been practicing. The skimming strategy allows you to focus on material that you do not wish to read closely. Since you might be searching for specific details, a quick scan of the material will give you an idea of what information it may contain and then a **careful skimming** of the material will lead you to the details in which you are interested.

Activity A. Interpreting Schedules

VUELO	DESTINO	SALIDA	EMBARQUE	PUERTA
345	Madrid	12:55	12:45	7
434	Valencia	15:55	15:45	5
645	Alicante	16:30	16:15	4
545	Sevilla	17:20	17:10	7
SALIDAS NACIONALES IBERIA				SALIDAS NACIONALES IBERIA

Now answer the following questions about the above schedule.

1. What is the mode of transportation?

2. What is the name of the company?

3. What cities are represented in the schedule?

4. What time should one be ready to leave if one is going to Madrid?

5. What does *salidas nacionales* refer to?

6. What does *puerta* mean?

As you move through the skimming process, try to find the topic sentence of each paragraph or segment of the material. The topic sentence focuses on the main idea and is a clue to understanding the details of the passage. Using all the pre-reading strategies that you have learned, you are now ready to read to get the gist of the material. The context clues, your knowledge of cognates, and the background knowledge that you bring to the reading process are key elements in reading for basic understanding. And, as always, take a risk and be ready to guess!

Activities for getting the gist of a passage.

Activity A. El mundo hispano connection! Take out your text and turn to page 13 and read the article on Miguel Angel Asturias. Write 5 facts that you learned from reading the passage.

Activity B. Again, using your text, turn to page 12 and read the passage "Pasatiempos y diversiones". Be sure to look for

cognates as you read to get the gist. Now, answer the following questions.

1. What country is being highlighted in the passage?

2. What are the people trying to preserve in their country?

3. How much land has been designated for natural preservation?

4. What does *ecoturismo* refer to?

Content Words and Function Words

Basically, **content words** are words that convey **meaning.** They refer to people, events, places, things, ideas, and concepts. You will notice that many content words are nouns, adjectives, verbs and, frequently, cognates. You will notice that the most important content words are often repeated, especially in ads, where it is important to make sure the reader is focusing on the product. As you work to develop your reading skills, you will most likely want to look for definitions of the unfamiliar content words that you come across in your reading. For now, use what you have learned about scanning and guessing.

Function words, on the other hand, are words that are used in a passage and are critical to total comprehension in that they tie thoughts together. Prepositions, articles, conjunctions, and auxiliaries are all function words and one must learn the meanings of these words to understand them. Function words are not that helpful in the pre-reading stage but take on greater significance in the interpretation and summary stages of the reading process.

Some good examples of function words that will help you in your reading are:

- Demonstrative adjectives and pronouns – *este, esta,* "this" *estos, estas*, "those," etc. *éste, ésta*, "this one," *éstos, éstas*, "those" etc.

- Possessive adjectives – *mi (s), tu (s), su (s), nuestro,a, (s), vuestro, a (s), su (s)* "my," "your," "his," "her," "its," "our," "your," "their."

- Conjunctions: *y* "and," *pero* "but," *sino* ("but" –after a negative)
- Definite and indefinite articles – *el, la, los, las* "the"
- Prepositions such as *a* "at, to," *de* "from, of" *en* "in," *por* "for through, by," *para* "in order to," *con* "with," *sin* "without," etc.

(See Appendix A for further examples and meanings.)

Activity A. Look at the following ads and underline all the content words. Many of these will be cognates.

HOTEL REYES DE SALAMANCA
Balneario
Precio por persona: $75 euros
Incluye: autocar + pensión completa, incluido vino. Guías, consultas médicas, tratamientos balneoterápicos con programa de animación
Teléfonos: 343 22 76 343 55 09

BRILLANTE
¡Pasta dental anticaries con Fluoristat!
Sabor menta
¡Úsela todos los días!

Part B. Now decide whether these words are especially important based on format cues or because they are repeated.

Activity B. Look at this passage and find the content words. Make a list on the opposite page and guess the meaning based on context.

Ropa elegante

La moda se hace para disfrutarla. Y todas las mujeres se merecen tener un conjunto elegante, de una tela que parece de cristal. Para la noche, María usa delicadísimas telas en las que abundan pequeñas cuentas de cristal. Los motivos se repiten en ligeras variaciones en los vestidos largos y los cortos. Es la clase de ropa elegante y de muy refinada sensualidad que usan muchas clientas de Armani, muchas de ellas son ejecutivas de intensa vida social. Estas mujeres buscan este tipo de ropa para ocasiones especiales después de las 5:00 de la tarde.

Activity C. Now read this passage and answer the following questions.

¡Al aire fresco!

Sentarse en la terraza de una casa logra en un instante una atmósfera de informalidad, muy conveniente para leer su libro favorito o celebrar una ocasión especial con unos amigos. La mejor adición que se le puede hacer a una casa es la terraza. No se necesita mucho espacio para construirla; se necesita nada más un poco de territorio del comedor, de la sala o del patio. A todos les va a gustar estar al aire fresco, no importa qué estación del año sea.

Una parte de la terraza puede estar rodeada de cristales, de modo que se pueda aislar del exterior en caso de que haga mucho frío o poner el aire acondicionado si hace mucho calor. Como prolongación de la casa, la terraza ofrece muchas posibilidades y su estilo puede ser más informal que el resto de los cuartos.

Sí, la mejor adición que se le puede hacer a una casa es la terraza. En esta pieza se puede estar en contacto con la naturaleza sin tener que estar fuera de la casa. Además, su cálida informalidad es ideal para la conversación.

1. What is the passage suggesting?

2. What are some of the benefits of this addition to one's home?

3. What type of atmosphere is created with this addition?

4. What does *estar en contacto con la naturaleza* mean?

5. What makes this room ideal for conversation with friends?

¡Un poco de todo! Read the following passages and answer the questions that follow.

"Comida de osos"

Daniel C. Weaver

El oso de las cavernas de la Edad Glacial en Europa era más grande que un oso polar. Pesaba más de 700 kilos y superaba los tres metros de altura. Pese a esas proporciones, los paleontólogos piensan que estos osos se alimentaban sólo de raíces y frutas. Sus dientes y huesos maxilares indican que su función era más la de moler vegetales que destrozar carne. Gran Hilderbrand, especialista de la Universidad Estatal de Washington, siempre se preguntaba cómo esos osos tan inmensos pudieron tener una dieta tan pobre en proteínas cuando un oso polar, que es más pequeño, necesita por lo menos 100 kilos de carne de foca al día para sobrevivir. Su escepticismo estaba bien fundamentado: ha descubierto que estos osos eran omnívoros y que tenían gran predilección por la carne.

¿Qué aprendiste? Answer the following questions based on the passage you have just read.

1. Underline all the cognates in the passage.
2. Make a list of the content words and function words.
3. You may not know the word "*oso*" without looking it up, but there is a clue as to its meaning (*oso polar*) in the body of the text. Using this cognate clue, what is an "*oso de las cavernas*"?
4. What was the typical diet of this animal? How was that determined?
5. Who is Gran Hilderbrand? What is his opinion on the matter?

En español…

1. Entonces, el oso de las cavernas era herbívoro, carnívoro u omnívoro?
2. ¿Cuántos kilos de carne necesita el oso polar para sobrevivir?

"Un viaje vital"

¿Cómo se desliza la sangre por nuestros cuerpos? En primer lugar, los estudios más aceptados sostienen que comienza a fluir desde el corazón, a través de la vena aorta. Después, la sangre se abre camino hacia las arterias y arteriolas de ramificaciones cada vez más complejas. A esa altura, la marcha se torna imparable hasta que desemboca en una elaborada red de canales, conocida como lecho capilar. Allí se encuentran tortuosos conductos que, según los cálculos de los especialistas, sumarían una extensión aproximada de 100.000 kilómetros. Es allí donde se produce el intercambio de oxígeno y dióxido de carbono que purifica nuestros órganos y nos mantiene con vida.

¿Qué aprendiste? Answer the following questions based on the passage you have just read.

1. In order to understand the passage, you need to know the word "*viaje*." From what infinitive is it derived?
2. Based on what you learned from the text, why does the author use the title *"Un viaje vital"*? It is in reference to what fundamental process in the human body? What are the cognate clues that help to answer this question?
3. Explain the reference to "*100.000 kilómetros*".

En español.

4. ¿Dónde comienza a fluir la sangre y qué la lleva?
5. ¿Cuál es el otro término para la red de canales?

“Contra los delitos cibernéticos”

Javier Montes

Los virus informáticos globales, la difusión de la pornografía infantil e incluso las actividades terroristas son algunos ejemplos de los nuevos delitos virtuales y sin fronteras que presentan una realidad difícil de controlar. Con el avance de la tecnología digital en los últimos años, ha surgido una nueva generación de delincuentes que expone a los gobiernos, las empresas y los individuos a estos peligros.

El teclado de una computadora puede ser una herramienta muy útil para el progreso de la humanidad; también se puede convertir en una poderosa arma capaz de producir enormes daños económicos, contra la infraestructura de servicios de un Estado o una empresa, o aun contra la integridad y la vida de las personas.

¿Qué aprendiste? Answer the following questions based on the passage that you have just read.

1. The word “*cibernéticos*” gives an important clue to the topic of the passage. To what does it refer?
2. “*Delitos*” is a false cognate! Read the passage again to deduce from the context what this word really means.
3. List the cognates that you found to be helpful in understanding the passage.
4. The cyber age has given way to what type of individual?
5. The passage indicates some of the dangers of misusing technology. What are some of these dangers?

En español…

6. En qué forma puede ser la computadora una herramienta útil?

"La educación: clave del desarrollo"

Los ministros de educación de todo el hemisferio afirmaron que en las próximas décadas, la educación debe convertirse en "la prioridad central del desarrollo" y pidieron que las nuevas estrategias aumenten la financiación disponible.

La III Reunión de Ministros de Educación, celebrada en la ciudad de México en el mes de agosto, puso de relieve el papel de la educación en la promoción de la equidad social, la lucha contra la pobreza y el fortalecimiento de los valores democráticos. Los ministros renovaron su compromiso de alcanzar los objetivos educativos establecidos en las Cumbres de las Américas, entre lo que se destaca el de garantizar que para el año 2010 todos los niños asistan a las escuelas primarias que provean una educación de alta calidad y que por lo menos el 75 por ciento de los jóvenes tenga acceso a la educación secundaria.

En la Declaración de México, afirmaron: "Nos hemos comprometido a educar a las generaciones presentes y futuras en sus capacidades para participar en un ambiente globalizado y lograr un hemisferio donde ningún niño quede rezagado."

¿Qué aprendiste? Answer the following questions based on the passage you have just read.

1. According to the article, what is the key to the development of a country?
2. Where did the 3rd Meeting of Ministers of Education take place and when?
3. What goals did the Ministers establish in their meeting?
4. In the context of the passage, what do the following phrases mean:
   a) "*puso de relieve el papel de la educación*"
   b) "*…un hemisferio donde ningún niño quede rezagado.*"

En español…

5. ¿A qué se han comprometido los ministros?

Lesson 4

THE DECODING PROCESS

You are now ready to read for details, using what you have learned about skimming, scanning, background knowledge, content words and function words. But, don't run for the dictionary yet! Because of the number of cognates in Spanish and the wealth of context clues, you will find it much easier to understand specific words and begin the decoding process.

The verb is the nucleus of the sentence and is critical to comprehension. Remember that a verb describes action, essence or being. Verbs in their basic form are called **infinitives** and always end in **–ar, -er,** and **-ir.** The root of the infinitive (all the letters preceding the infinitive ending) is often derived from Latin so the root combined with the ending gives you the whole infinitive. Here are some examples of infinitives: *practicar, estudiar, comer, ver, recibir, escribir.* Can you tell what they mean?

Further decoding delves into the study of prefixes, suffixes and roots. (Remember the lesson on cognates?) There are many prefixes in Spanish that give you significant clues as to the meaning of words. Some of these are: *a-, des-, en-, de-, re-, com-, su-, ob-,* etc. Suffixes are added to the word as endings that convey specific ideas and allow the formation of many new words from the root. Some of these are:

-ito/ita, illo, illa – diminutive indicating small in size or denoting affection
-ón/ona – augmentative or negative connotation
-ote/ota – large size or negative connotation
-eza – added to an adjective to form a feminine noun
-dad, -tad – equivalent to –ty in English
-ería – denotes a place where something is made or sold
-ero/era – indicates a person who makes, sells or is in charge of
-ía – ending for many arts and sciences

-mente – is the adverbial ending, typically attached to the feminine form of the adjective

Activity A. With your dictionary in hand, see if you can define the following words, keeping in mind the information about prefixes and suffixes that you have just studied.

1. *perrito*________________	6. *casita*_____________
2. *zapatero*______________	7. *liberta*_____________
3. *biología*________________	8. *felizmente*__________
4. *deshacer*______________	9. *librote*_____________
5. *hombrón*______________	10. *enriquecer*_________

Close Reading

The term **close reading** means that you are now ready to carefully consider what you are reading, paragraph by paragraph or segment by segment as in a detailed ad, announcement, article or longer text. With the pre-reading strategies you considered format, cues, and context to determine meaning. In the decoding process you practiced extracting specific meaning, being attentive to structural details and content. These strategies work well with simple, straight-forward information.

Remember that reading is an interactive process that often calls for a reaction, opinion or emotional response on the part of the reader--you! This response requires that you identify and evaluate the writer's tone, point- of- view and message. These more complex passages require greater attention to detail and comprehension. In this type of reading, there will be a range of vocabulary and complex structures

Activity A. Read the following paragraph using the reading strategies that you have been practicing and then answer the following questions.

"Algo para ellos"

¿Qué es el perfume? Ah, el perfume siempre ha sido el regalo que más nos gusta recibir, no importa cuándo. Siempre hay algo evocador en todos los perfumes; su esencia nos lleva a mundos aparte, mundos de misterio, sensualidad, sensaciones. El regalo de un perfume nos hace pensar: «¿A quién se lo damos?». A una amiga joven y activa, por ejemplo, claro que le gustará uno fresco y suave que huela a una fruta como la naranja o el limón. También hay unos perfumes que son aún más fuertes, exóticos, de rosas y jazmines, que se dejan para la noche en una ocasión especial. Es el regalo perfecto para una mujer ejecutiva o de intensa vida social. Si la persona no es una amiga íntima y hay que escoger, decídase por los clásicos y de moda. La compra de un buen perfume dice que "Pensé en ti al escoger esta esencia."

¿Y para el hombre? Sorpréndale con un buen perfume de hombre. Muchos de ellos se hacen ahora con más frutas y flores pero, al mismo tiempo, sus aromas son muy masculinos. Para el hombre distinguido, cómprele uno de los clásicos. Finalmente, para el hombre de sus sueños, cómprele el que más le guste a usted porque es usted quien lo va a disfrutar.

1. What is the topic of this reading?

2. What kind of advice is given regarding this product?

3. Who can benefit from a gift of this nature?

4. What is meant by *los clásicos?*

5. Does this article inspire you to go and purchase this product for someone?

Contesta en español.

6. ¿Quién va a disfrutar más el perfume del hombre?

7. ¿De qué se hacen muchos perfumes?

8. ¿Cuál es el perfume perfecto para una mujer joven y activa?

Activity B. El mundo hispano connection! Turn to page 17 in your text. Read the article on "Arte" and then answer the following questions.

1. List at least 10 cognates.

2. What is the topic sentence?

3. Where can one find many of the works of Diego Rivera?

4. Frida Kahlo is famous for what type of artwork?

En español…

5. ¿En qué se inspiraba Diego Rivera?

6. ¿Cómo son muchas de las obras de Frida?

7. Describe la relación entre Diego y Frida.

8. ¿Qué aspectos caracterizan las obras de Diego Rivera?

Activity C. ¡*Consejos!* Many newspapers and magazines carry advice columns. See what Magda has to offer her clients in the following texts.

Querida Magda:
Soy una mujer muy bonita e inteligente, con bastante dinero pero no tengo novio en este momento. Normalmente, tengo mucho éxito con los hombres pero no sé lo que me pasa ahora. Sí, me respetan y me dicen que me aprecian pero nunca están listos para enamorarse de mí; nada más quieren ser amigos. Estoy desesperada porque no quiero muchos amigos, ¡quiero un esposo!

Espero que Ud. me pueda ayudar.

Tania

Querida Magda:
Tengo un problema muy serio.
Cuando me casé con mi esposa hace dos años, me dijo que no quería trabajar fuera de la casa porque quería cuidar a nuestros niños. Ahora que tenemos un niñito de un año, me dice que quiere salir a trabajar. Creo que esto es injusto porque habíamos decidido que no iba a trabajar ella. Dice que no quiere estar en casa cambiando pañales y haciendo los quehaceres. ¿Qué sugiere?

Arturo

Querida Magda:
Soy mexicana con un problema que es muy típico. Vengo de una familia muy tradicional y mis papás no quieren que yo estudie en la universidad. Dicen que necesito buscar un buen marido y tener una familia grande. No quiero casarme hasta los 35 años o más. Quiero estudiar letras y luego ser profesora en la UNAM. ¿Qué me aconseja? Estoy desesperada.

Susana

¡En español! Escribe el número de las siguientes personas que se describen en estas cartas.

1. Susana 2. Los papás de Susana 3. Tania

4. Arturo 5. La esposa de Arturo

A. Tienen ideas conservadoras.
B. No tiene un novio que quiera casarse con ella.
C. Quiere estudiar en la universidad.
D. No le gusta la idea de estar en casa todo el día con los niños.
E. Tiene una familia muy tradicional.
F. Es bonita e inteligente pero no tiene con quién casarse.
G. Es algo conservador; no quiere que su esposa trabaje fuera de casa.
H. No está contenta con su vida como ama de casa.
I. Tiene un plan con su esposa que ella quiere rechazar.

Activity D. *¡El horóscopo!* Read the following predictions and see if you can answer the questions that follow.

Aries (marzo 21 a abril 19)

- El tránsito de Venus le es propicio y a su favor. Tiene la gran oportunidad de su vida: viajar a un país exótico. El espíritu acuariano le está guiando. No se rebele y piénselo bien. El dinero necesario llegará. Conocerá a nuevos amigos y tal vez una alianza romántica le llegue.

Tauro (abril 20 a mayo 20)

- No piense que el amor se ha ido para siempre. Venus, que es el protector del amor, llega con muy buenas noticias para este signo. Es un período muy positivo para dar inicio a nuevos proyectos y amistades. No desaproveche ninguna oportunidad que se presente.

Géminis (mayo 21 a junio 21)

- Su deseo de triunfar y aprovecharse de las oportunidades está en su máxima expresión en estos días. Reconozca estas oportunidades y póngase a trabajar. También, busque diferentes soluciones para resolver unos problemas familiares que se presentarán durante estos días.

Cáncer (junio 22 a julio 22)

- La luna está llena en su signo. Esta es una influencia cósmica y hay que aprovecharla. Tendrá noticias muy positivas al respecto de una cantidad de dinero que le va a llegar muy pronto. Esta es la etapa de las buenas inversiones. ¡Felicidades! El futuro le pertenece.

Now, match the following predictions with the corresponding astrological sign.

- Be ready for love.
- Money is in your future.
- Many positive opportunities will come your way.
- It's a good time to start a variety of projects.
- It's a full moon and cosmic energy abounds.
- There is a love match in your future.
- There are some opportunities for some good investments.
- Take advantage of every opportunity that presents itself.
- It's time to go to work.
- Travel is in your future.
- It's time to seek solutions to some family problems.

Activity E. El mundo hispano connection. Turn to page 27 in this text and read the article entitled *Cocina.* Be sure to look for cognates and details that will help you to understand more fully what you are reading. Now answer the following questions.

1. How would one describe Caribbean cuisine?

2. What are the most common meats used in this this type of cooking?

3. What is the most characteristic dish in the Caribbean?

4. What is the most popular fruit? Describe the different types of this fruit?

En español…

5. ¿Qué otros tipos de platos se aprecian mucho en el Caribe?

6. ¿Cómo se prepara la banana?

Activity F. *¡A comer!* Read this article that has to do with a very popular Mexican food. You will need to use all the reading strategies that you have learned because there are many details in this text. ¡Buena suerte!

"Una comida muy mexicana"

Susana Aguirre Hernández

Alrededor de la República Mexicana se puede encontrar un gran mosaico de sabores en lo que a tamales se refiere. Hay salados acompañados de carne, algunas verduras y salsas. También hay tamales dulces con frutas y semillas que les dan un toque característico.

En los estados de Chiapas, Tabasco, Yucatán, Oaxaca, Veracruz y Michoacán y otros, hay una variedad infinita de tamales con ingredientes tales como chile verde y rojo, mole, frijol, queso, nata, cacahuate, pollo, carne de cerdo, pescado, nopales y más. Pero el chile estará presente siempre como el ingrediente principal. Los tamales dulces contienen nuez, pasitas, piña, coco, ciruela pasa y otras frutas frescas y secas.

La forma de envolver el tamal es también muy variada. Se usan hojas de maíz y hojas de elote secas. Las hojas de plátano se usan principalmente en la zona costera o tropical.

Para acompañar los tamales, se acostumbran bebidas calientes como el atole. El atole se hace de harina o masa de maíz blanco molido con leche o sin ella, con miel, azúcar, piloncillo, canela, vainilla, almendra, nuez y frutas, como ciruela pasa, guayaba, fresa, tamarindo, tuna y coco. También se acostumbra el champurrado, atole hecho con agua, maíz, chocolate y piloncillo. Hay otra bebida muy popular y es el café de olla, endulzado y con canela. ¡Buen provecho!

Now answer the following questions.

1. Write five things that you learned about the preparation of tamales.

2. What does one use to wrap the tamales that are made on the coast?

3. How many varieties of tamales are there?

4. What are some of the ingredients that are used to prepare tamales?

En español...

5. ¿Qué se bebe cuando se comen los tamales?

6. ¿Cuáles son los ingredientes del champurrado?

7. ¿Qué contienen los tamales dulces?

8. ¿Cuál es tu tamal favorito?

Activity G. ¡*Una receta!* Using your background knowledge, you will immediately recognize the format of the following text. Read closely to understand what is required to produce this pastel azteca.

Pastel Azteca

La dieta del mexicano se basa en el maíz y las tortillas son imprescindibles.

INGREDIENTES

- Un kilo de tortillas de maíz
- Una pechuga de pollo cocida y desmenuzada
- 2 chiles poblanos asados y pelados
- 2 elotes desgranados
- 150 gr de queso manchego
- 200 ml de crema
- ½ kg de jitomate
- 2 dientes de ajo picados
- 4 cucharadas de cebolla picada
- 2 calabacitas picadas
- una ramita de epazote
- sal y pimienta al gusto

MODO DE PREPARARSE

Se fríen las tortillas de maíz. En otra sartén, se acitrona un diente de ajo y dos cucharadas de cebolla. Se agregan las calabazas, los elotes y las rajas de chile poblano. Se baja la flama y se pone el epazote. Se sazona y se tapa. Se deja en el fuego hasta que los elotes estén bien cocidos; entonces, se agrega el pollo.

En una sartén, se pone una cucharadita de aceite y se vacía el jitomate licuado con ajo y cebolla. La salsa se deja hervir unos minutos hasta que espese.

En un refractario, se acomodan las tortillas y después el relleno de verduras y luego se baña la salsa de jitomate. Este procedimineto se repite hasta llenar el molde. Por último, se decora con crema y queso. Se hornea a 200 grados centígrados hasta que el queso gratine.

Now answer the following questions.

1. Obviously, this is a ________________ to make ________________.

2. What ingredients do you recognize without using your dictionary?

3. What are the important verbs in the process of preparation?

4. If you intend to make this dish and you want it to be a success, you will need to get your dictionary and use the dictionary strategies that you have learned and practiced. Look up the key words necessary to understand this recipe.

5. Is this dish baked or fried? Which verb tells you this? What noun is derived from this verb?

   After you have studied this text and feel that you understand fully what it is you need to do, why not attempt to make it and share it with your friends and family?

¡Un poco de todo! Read the following passages and answer the questions that follow.

"Los vikingos"
Kathy Svitil

Siempre se ha dicho que Cristóbal Colón fue el primer europeo que llegó al Nuevo Mundo con el fin de conquistar nuevas tierras para la corona española. Sin embargo, restos arqueológicos encontrados en los extremos septentrionales de Norteamérica han revelado que, en realidad, los primeros europeos que pisaron lo que después sería América fueron los rubios hombres del norte europeo. No dejaron una huella permanente en América, pero su paso por el norte de Europa afectó profundamente la historia del

Viejo Mundo así como su actual conformación étnica. Los vikingos eran guerreros paganos que llegaron desde los gélidos territorios escandinavos impulsados a la conquista del continente por una combinación de factores entre los que se incluyen la sobrepoblación y la escasa resistencia que encontraron entre los pueblos más atrasados del norte de Europa. En sus territorios, los vikingos eran agricultores y comerciantes independientes que en los viajes de conquista se convertían en excelentes navegantes y guerreros que extendieron sus dominios en todo el norte del continente, a la región báltica y lo que hoy es Rusia. Además de su carácter aventurero, los vikingos legaron a los pueblos conquistados un idioma cuyas raíces unen especialmente a los habitantes de lo que son Dinamarca, Noruega y Suecia.

¿Qué aprendiste? Answer the following questions based on the passage you just read.

1. Go through the passage and list the cognates that will help you to understand the topic.
2. Underline the verb forms and indicate the infinitive from which each is derived.
3. Using the Appendix A, identify the tense of the verb forms that you have found.
4. The word "*guerrero*" may be unfamiliar to you but you may know the word "*guerra*". What is the connection?
5. At first, the Vikings were considered to be what kind of people? How is it that they came to be known as fierce warriors?

En español.

6. ¿Describe el carácter de los vikingos?
7. ¿Qué legaron los vikingos a los pueblos conquistados?
8. ¿Se asocian los vikingos con cuáles países?

"En lo alto de Caracas"

Larry Luxner

Después de quince años de abandono, el teleférico de Caracas está funcionando nuevamente, una buena noticia para los turistas y residentes de la capital venezolana.

Hace cinco años, el consorcio privado Inversora Turística Caracas S.A. obtuvo una concesión de tres años para manejar el funicular que une Caracas con el hotel Humboldt, ubicado en la cima del cerro, El Ávila, a una altura de 2.153 metros sobre el nivel del mar.

El Humboldt, un cilindro de doce pisos y 60 metros de altura que en un día despejado puede verse desde cualquier punto de Caracas, había sido abandonado desde su cierre en 1987, por la misma época en que dejó de pasar el teleférico estatal, que funcionó desde 1956 hasta principios de los setenta y después durante un breve período a mediados de los ochenta.

El funicular – cuya capacidad alcanza los dos mil pasajeros por hora y se eleva 1.111 metros en sólo 3,5 kilómetros de distancia – fue construido por Dopelmayr Cable Car GmbH, un fabricante austriaco que ha instalado casi trescientos funiculares en sesenta y ocho países, entre los que se incluyen Colombia, Costa Rica, Brasil y España.

¿Qué aprendiste? Answer the following questions based on the passage you just read.

1. Caracas is the capital of what country?
2. What mode of transportation has attracted tourists to the city?
3. Where is it and what is its name?

4. What do you notice about the way numbers and decimals are written in the article?
5. What happened to it in 1987?
6. Who is particularly pleased with the repair of this mode of transportation?
7. Exactly what is "*un funicular*"?

En español…

8. ¿A cuántos pasajeros puede acomodar el funicular cada hora?
9. ¿Qué compañía construyó el funicular?
10. ¿En cuántos países se encuentran los funiculares construidos por esta compañía?

"El nuevo museo del niño"

Randy Schultz

El nuevo Museo del Niño de Copán Ruinas en el norte de Honduras brinda a los jóvenes la posibilidad de aprender sobre su cultura en tres idiomas--inglés, español y chortí--y está atrayendo a una creciente cantidad de visitantes internacionales a esta relativamente aislada región.

El internacionalmente reconocido arqueólogo Ricardo Agurcia, fundador y director de la Asociación Copán, encabezó un esfuerzo por aumentar el conocimiento del rico patrimonio de la región y su potencial de desarrollo.

¿Qué aprendiste? Answer the following questions based on the passage that you just read.

1. What does the passage describe?
2. Where is this place and what is its significance?
3. You know the word "*cabeza*" so what does the verb "*encabezó*" mean?

En español…

4. ¿Por qué es tan importante este museo?
5. ¿De quién fue la idea de establecer el museo y a quién se ha dedicado?

"El universo y la informática"

Margaret A. Boden

Cuando un grupo de astrofísicos quiso simular las interacciones de una galaxia pensaron que el programa informático más avanzado podía ayudarles. Pero se enfrentaron a la inmensidad inimaginable del universo. La operación necesita 10.000 millones de cálculos simples de aritmética. Si se toma en cuenta que hay unos 30 millones de segundos en un año y que el programa informático más rápido podía realizar 100 millones de operaciones en un segundo, una sola simulación galáctica demoraría 3.000 años. Sin duda ésta sería una espera demasiado larga, dijo un descorazonado miembro del grupo de astrofísicos.

¿Qué aprendiste? Answer the following questions based on the passage you have just read.

1. What are the astrophysicists trying to figure out?
2. How many arithmetical calculations are necessary to answer their questions?
3. Why would it take 3,000 years to make one galactic simulation?

En español…

4. Al descubrir la cantidad de tiempo que tomaría para solucionar su problema, ¿cómo reaccionaron los científicos?

Lesson 5

SUMMARIZING AND CROSS-REFERENCING

Another important reading strategy is **summarizing** and **cross-referencing.** The key element here is the ability to recognize **context, topic sentences** and **key words.** Again, when it comes to context, you can draw on your extensive background knowledge to help in comprehension. Remember that you bring a depth of knowledge from your native language (L1) to everything you read in the second language. (L2)

You will first notice the use of **specific language** related to the main topic. For example, if you are trying to decode material having to do with computer technology, you will key in on specific vocabulary dealing with this topic. If you are reading material related to country profiles, you will then be aware of vocabulary, structures and format that support this topic. As you decode, it is very helpful to stop and summarize in your own words what you have just read, reducing the content to a few main ideas and using words that convey the central meaning of the passage.

Look at the following text:

> **ARTE Museo. Con un año de adquisiciones, donaciones y recuperaciones, el Museo Nacional de Arte de Cataluña muestra las más significativas piezas ingresadas como fondo del museo en el último período. A destacar, la inclusión de dos esculturas de Julio González, legadas por su hija al museo.**

Using the decoding and summarizing process, you could say that **the National Museum of Art of Cataluña is including two sculptures by Julio González in their exhibit.** This, then, is a brief summary of the passage.

Activity A. Summarize the following passage in your own words. Be sure to look for the topic sentence and use it as your guide to summarize the content.

¡Nuestro nuevo amigo infatigable!

¿Qué sabes de las primeras computadoras? ¿Jamás has pensado en su origen y su desarrollo? Puede ser que mucha gente no considere la historia de esta máquina tan útil porque ahora es algo tan conocida, usada y necesaria en la vida diaria que muchos de nosotros no podríamos imaginar cómo sería la vida sin ella.

Según los expertos, la primera computadora electrónica ocupaba el espacio equivalente a 10 cocheras, pesaba 30 toneladas y al encenderla gastaba tanta energía que no se usaba mucho. La máquina era tan grande y producía tanto calor que se veía como un monstruo ineficaz aunque podía sumar 5 mil números por segundo. En comparación con las computadoras actuales, ¡ese dinosauro era lentísimo!

Siempre ha habido una fascinación con las máquinas para realizar operaciones de manera más rápida y fácil. A partir del ábaco, se han creado diferentes máquinas manuales y electrónicas para lograr esa rapidez y eficiencia en las operaciones matemáticas.

Las primeras computadoras se utilizaban para calcular la ruta de los proyectiles de guerra y tenían un uso muy limitado. Pero en la actualidad, son instrumentos que nos facilitan la vida de mil maneras. Vamos al cajero automático para retirar dinero--una computadora facilita esa operación. Nos divertimos con las películas que emplean efectos especiales engendrados por computadoras. También se usan para crear sistemas de seguridad y para realizar cientos de operaciones técnicas. Con la red mundial, es posible mandar y recibir miles de mensajes, fotos, anuncios y buscar información sin límite. ¡Toda una biblioteca está a su alcance!

Explore su mundo a través de esta máquina mágica y aprenda cómo aprovecharla en su beneficio. ¡Verá qué amigable y útil es!

Activity B. El mundo hispano connection! Let's try some more summaries. Read the following texts and write a brief summary of each one.

Page 32 Mario Vargas Llosa

Page 35 Gente y sociedad

Page 36 Personaje eminente

Cross-Referencing

Another critical element in the decoding process is the use of the cross-referencing strategies. In any type of passage, whether in L1 or L2, it is customary to avoid constant repetition of nouns. Instead, synonyms and other grammatical devices are used. These words are references to the nouns in the passage.

Now, scan the following passage about Rigoberta Menchú and pay close attention to the use of cross references.

Rigoberta Menchú, indígena maya-quiché, luchadora por los derechos humanos y defensora de la gente indígena, ganó el Premio Nóbel de la Paz en 1992. Esta mujer extraordinaria nació en 1959 y desde muy joven comenzó a luchar por su gente. Se dedicó a una labor infatigable para mejorar la condición social indígena en Guatemala.

After reading this short passage about Rigoberta Menchú, the Nobel Prize winner from Guatemala, you will have noticed that besides using her name, there were references to Rigoberta as *indígena maya-quiché, luchadora, defensora, esta mujer extraordinaria, ella* and the like. These are all cross-references that refer to Rigoberta Menchú without having to repeat her name. As you develop your reading skills, you will make note of all the cross-references while you summarize what you have read.

There are grammatical elements for cross-referencing as well. These are pronouns, possessives and demonstratives. In the article on Rigoberta, you see the use of *ella*, *esta mujer*, etc., elements which show a definite relationship to the main topic, Rigoberta Menchú. In regard to pronouns that are used as cross-references, you must be aware of the patterns of direct and indirect object pronouns in Spanish. These are used extensively in both spoken and written language to avoid repetition and ambiguity.

Activity A. Using the grammatical appendix as your guide, find the pronouns in this passage and underline them. See if you can give their meaning as well.

Mi novia, María, es muy simpática pero a veces no me gustan sus acciones. Yo la encuentro un poco celosa y eso sí me molesta. A ella no le gusta hacer lo que a mí me gusta. Es decir que yo soy muy activo pero ella es bastante sedentaria. Mis amigos me dicen que debo de dejarla, pero no puedo; todavía la amo mucho.

Metaphors

In your close reading, you must also be aware of the use of **metaphors,** which are an indirect way of referring to nouns by making associations that are not normally attributed to a noun. These references are not to be taken literally; they are often allusions made to enhance the creativity of the passage. A careful reader will be able to enjoy the visual imaging and sophisticated language the writer uses. Much of what you read will have cultural associations as well, adding to the richness of your reading experience.

Idioms

As you work with more difficult reading passages, you will become aware of phrases that have no literal translation. These are called **idioms** and are often used metaphorically to enrich the spoken and written language. Knowing the individual meanings of the words in such phrases is not helpful because idioms are fixed phrases whose individual elements have no meaning. Imaginative writing is replete with idiomatic expressions.

There are many such expressions in L1 and the same idea will be expressed very differently in L2. It is important to know the meaning of the whole phrase in order to be successful in the decoding of such expressions. Again, be aware of the context in which the idiom is used; this helps to understand the reference.

For example, a common weather idiom in English is: "It's raining cats and dogs." Now, this is not to be taken literally. Spanish has an idiom to express the same idea, but it has nothing to do with cats and dogs! *Llover a cántaros* is the expression in Spanish. A *cántaro* is a pitcher or a jug. Get the connection?

Another expression in English is: "You're pulling my leg." The speaker, we assume, has not touched the other person's leg; he is merely using the expression to indicate that the whole truth is not being told, i.e., it's a joke. In Spanish, the expression would be: *Me estás tomando el pelo.* Though the idea is the same, Spanish uses "pulling hair" instead of "pulling the leg."

Again, idioms are very interesting and make use of a variety of words that are juxtaposed in a phrase without attention to literal meanings; they must be learned in the context in which they are used.

Activity A. For the Spanish idioms listed below, give their literal meaning in English. Then check your dictionary and give a good English translation equivalent.

1. *sudar la gota gorda*

2. *meter la cuchara*

3. *no tener pelos en la lengua*

4. *poner el grito en el cielo*

5. *dar calabazas*

Activity B. Listed below are some common expressions or idioms in Spanish. See if you can match them with a similar idiom in English.

1. *en traje de Adán*	A. to be in one's element
2. *en un dos por tres*	B. to have a super time
3. *estar en su mero mole*	C. not by a long shot!
4. *es otro cantar*	D. to be stuck up, put on airs
5. *echar sapos y culebras*	E. as harmless as a fly
6. *divertirse en grande*	F. to swear a blue streak
7. *darse mucho taco*	G. in your dreams!
8. *inocente como una paloma*	H. in the wink of an eye
9. *¡Ni soñar!*	I. in one's birthday suit
10. *trato hecho*	J. It's quite a feast!
11. *por las buenas o las malas*	K. By hook or by crook!
12. *zapatero a tus zapatos*	L. Mind your own business!
13. *una comilona*	M. It's a deal!

¡Un poco de todo! Read the following passages and answer the questions that follow.

"Rock and Roll en español"
Mark Holston

El centro de gravedad está desplazándose. Por momentos, el cambio ha tenido la fuerza de un huracán. En un mundo en el que las arraigadas tradiciones constituían en una época una que no cuestionaba, está surgiendo un nuevo panorama musical que se basa en la insatisfacción con el status quo y una actitud conscientemente irreverente que ha captado la imaginación de una generación para la que los boleros, la salsa, la samba y los tangos de sus padres y abuelos están tan desactualizados como una tarjeta postal en la época del correo electrónico.

Lo que comenzó como un movimiento musical basado casi exclusivamente en el lenguaje del rock internacional, ha evolucionado en algo más original que refleja las diversas culturas nacionales que han alimentado sus exponentes más creativos. En el proceso, la nueva música se ha convertido en una verdadera alternativa a la que la precedió y al mismo tiempo, en cierta forma irónicamente, ha comenzado a reexaminar las formas tradicionales y a incorporar ciertos elementos de la música que en una época se consideraba pasada de moda. Ya no se trata solamente de jóvenes iracundos armados exclusivamente de guitarras electrónicas; ahora son músicos serios con bajo sextos, congas y trompetas.

Ya no se trata de un movimiento marginal confinado a los antros bohemios de las grandes zonas urbanas y los campus de las grandes universidades, lo que hasta no hace mucho tiempo se denominaba rock en español se ha convertido en un movimiento cultural y musicalmente diverso que está atrayendo la atención mundial.

¿Qué aprendiste? Answer the following questions based on the passage you have just read.

1. What are some of the characteristics that defined rock and roll at its inception and how has this genre evolved and changed?
2. What is the comparison that the author makes between the musicians in the early development of rock and roll and those of today?
3. Look at the passage again and list some of the cross-referencing elements that you have been studying in this chapter. (synonyms, pronouns, possessives, demonstratives, etc.)

En español...

4. ¿En qué se basa este nuevo panorama musical?

¡Una sorpresa!

Un director de un banco conoció a una joven actriz que trabajaba en el teatro. Los dos se hicieron muy amigos y pronto el director le pidió que se casara con él; ella accedió encantada.

Sin embargo, el director tenía ciertas dudas sobre la conducta de su futura esposa porque las actrices suelen llevar una vida algo alegre: conocen a muchos hombres y salen con unos y con otros. Por eso, decidió encargar a una agencia de investigación que investigara sobre la vida de su novia.

Después de unas semanas, el detective privado encargado de la investigación le envió por correo el siguiente informe:

"La señorita Martín ha llevado siempre una vida ejemplar. Es conocida por todo el mundo como una chica decente y honesta. Sólo en los últimos tiempos se la ha visto acompañada de un individuo de profesión banquero, que tiene fama de ladrón y sinvergüenza."

¿Qué comprendiste?

1. First, make a list of all the cognates that you found in the story.
2. Underline the verbs and identify their tenses.
3. List at least 10 content words.
4. Whom did the bank manager meet? What did he propose?
5. Why did he hire a private detective?
6. What kind of a person is the young woman? And the bank manager?

En español…

7. ¿Por qué tienen mala fama las actrices?
8. ¿Cumplió el detective con su deber?

Lesson 6

Summary Activities

This final lesson will serve to give you the extra practice you need to demonstrate what you have learned about reading strategies in Spanish. These passages are taken from magazines and other texts; you should find them both informative and entertaining. Use the dictionary techniques that you have studied to fully understand what you are reading. And don't forget to focus on the cognates first!

Un poco de todo...

Activity A. Read the following passages and write a brief summary (two sentences) of what you learned. Remember, a summary is NOT a translation!

"Con muchos usos"

¿Quién dijo que la filosofía no tiene usos prácticos? Las sociedades se han visto profundamente afectadas por el pensamiento. La política se ha basado en muchas de las ideas de los filósofos clásicos griegos; la democracia y la ciudadanía son invenciones filosóficas; Marx y Engels contribuyeron como ningún otro personaje a la configuración del mundo del siglo XX; el positivismo de los años 20 impulsó el avance de la ciencia y el sistema binario, por el que funcicnan las computadoras, se basa en la lógica matemática, que no es otra cosa que una de las disciplinas de la filosofía.

Activity A. Passage 2

"En defensa del océano"

Los cruceros transportan millones de personas a lugares exóticos de las Américas. A medida que crece la industria, también crece el tamaño de los barcos. Algunos transportan hasta 5.000 pasajeros y tripulantes. Según un estudio realizado por G.P. Wild, para el año 2010 el número de pasajeros de cruceros aumentará a aproximadamente veintiún millones. El Caribe es el principal destino, y representa casi la mitad de todo el tráfico de cruceros.

El problema, según Oceana, una organización sin fines de lucro con sede en Washington, D.C, es que los cruceros tienen permiso para arrojar al océano desperdicios sin procesarlos. Para hacer frente a este problema, Oceana ha lanzado una campaña que procura detener la contaminación provocada por los cruceros con dos objetivos en mente: abogar por leyes federales en los Estados Unidos que controlen la contaminación del agua por parte de los cruceros y convencer a las empresas de que instalen equipos modernos de tratamiento de aguas residuales.

Activity A. Passage 3

"La verdadera edad del dios de los báculos"

Los investigadores del valle del río Patavilca, en el Perú, han encontrado un fragmento de vasija de cuatro mil años que parece ser el objeto religioso más antiguo de las Américas. El fragmento tiene la imagen del dios de los báculos, que era la principal figura religiosa en América del Sur hasta la llegada de los europeos en 1532. La datación radiocarbónica ha determinado que la vasija es del año 2250 antes de Cristo, y sugiere que la religión organizada comenzó en las Américas aproximadamente mil años antes que lo que se creía.

Activity A. Passage 4

"Llegan los supermexicanos"

En la Universidad Iberoamericana, José Martínez Quijada ha desarrollado por más de dos años un mini-robot como proyecto de tesis para obtener el título de Ingeniero en Electrónica y Comunicaciones. *Bart I* es el nombre de este ingenio que consta de 258 partes en un volumen aproximado de 83.8 cm3 y que incorpora 4 baterías recargables, las cuales proporcionan una hora de autonomía. Bautizado con el nombre del travieso primogénito de los *Simpson*, puede controlarse desde una PC por medio de un enlace de radio a 150MHz y también enviar datos hacia su estación de control o a otros robots. De carácter modulable, el mini-robot puede desarrollar diferentes tareas. La primera de ellas ha sido seguir una línea blanca sobre fondo negro. En la programación de esta actividad ha intervenido Juan Manuel Rosas Pineda, otro alumno de la universidad mencionada.

Activity A. Passage 5

"El origen de los antibióticos"

Aunque los antibióticos son sustancias que penetran la tierra de forma natural a través de las bacterias y los hongos, no llamaron la atención del mundo hasta la aparición de la penicilina en 1941. Desde entonces, han revolucionado el tratamiento de las infecciones bacterianas. En 1928, Alexander Fleming descubrió que un moho llamado *Penicillium Notatum* había contaminado a una colonia de bacterias que crecían en un cultivo de gérmenes. Diez años después, Ernst Chain y Howard Florey aislaron el ingrediente que había sido responsable: la penicilina. Demostraron que era efectiva en la lucha contra las infecciones bacterianas.

Activity B. Más cuentos. Read the following stories and answer the questions that follow.

"El automóvil y el tren"

Un automóvil se paró ante una barrera que había junto a la vía del tren. Esperó más de diez minutos, pero, al fin la barrera se levanta para permitir que pasen los coches.

Sin embargo, como el automovilista no había visto pasar ningún tren, se acercó al encargado de la barrera y le dijo:

---Oiga, perdone, ¿ha pasado algún tren? Porque yo no lo he visto.

El encargado de la barrera le contestó tranquilo:

---¿Que si ha pasado algún tren? ¡Ah, no! Hoy no pasan los trenes; el sindicato de empleados y trabajadores ha decretado huelga.

---Entonces, ¿por qué ha bajado usted la barrera impidiendo pasar los coches?

---Porque nuestro sindicato no ha ordenado ninguna huelga y era la hora de que pasara el tren que va de Barcelona a Madrid.

¿Qué comprendiste?

1. What happened when the driver got to the train crossing?
2. How long did he wait for the train to pass?
3. Whom did he consult to find out about the train?
4. How did the gatekeeper explain the situation?

En español...

1. ¿En qué país está viajando el automovilista?
2. ¿Qué es una "*huelga*"?

"El presidente y su pueblo"

El presidente de una república hispanoamericana quiso saber *hasta qué punto* le apreciaba su pueblo. Y disfrazándose con un bigote y unas gafas, salió a la calle vestido de obrero.

Después de pasear un rato comprobando que nadie le reconocía, decidió entrar en un cine. Antes de la película, apareció en las noticias el propio presidente, pronunciando un discurso; la gente inmediatamente se puso a aplaudir con gran entusiasmo. Todos, menos el propio presidente, que permanecía sentado, sin aplaudir, disfrutando de la popularidad de que gozaba entre su pueblo.

Pero, de pronto, el vecino que ocupaba el asiento de al lado le *llamó la atención* y le dijo en voz baja:

---Aplaude, imbécil, ¿o es que quieres que nos lleven a todos a la cárcel por tu culpa?

¿Qué comprendiste?

1. What do the expressions in italics mean?
2. What are the infinitives of the following words?
   a) pronunciando
   b) disfrutando
   c) disfrazándose
3. What does "*el propio presidente*" mean?
4. Why did the president disguise himself?

En español...

5. ¿ Le reconoció alguien en la calle?
6. ¿Qué pasó en el cine cuando el presidente apareció en las noticias?
7. ¿Qué hizo él?
8. ¿Qué habría pasado si el presidente no hubiera aplaudido?

Otro cuento...

"¿El profesor sabio?"

En una escuela el profesor trataba de explicarles a los alumnos lo malo que era para la salud beber alcohol.

Para demostrárselo de una manera práctica llevó dos vasos, uno con agua y otro con ginebra.

---Prestad mucha atención---les dijo el profesor a los alumnos---a lo que voy a hacer---y echó un gusano en cada uno de los vasos. ---Fijaos que en el vaso con agua el gusano sigue viviendo, mientras que en el vaso con ginebra, el gusano muere. ¿Qué consecuencias debemos sacar de este hecho?---añadió, dirigiéndose a uno de los alumnos más inteligentes de la clase.

---Esto nos enseña---contestó el alumno muy satisfecho de sí mismo---que, si no queremos tener gusanos en el estómago, tenemos que beber ginebra en vez de agua.

¿Que comprendiste?

1. How do you know that this story takes place in Spain?
2. What is "*ginebra*"?
3. What is a "*gusano*"?
4. Describe the experiment that the professor was using to demonstrate the evils of too much drinking?
5. Did the class get the point? Why or why not?

En español...

6. ¿Qué te parece el alumno que contestó la pregunta del profesor? ¿Cómo es?
7. Describe la reacción del profesor.

* * * * * * * * *

El que comienza bien, termina bien.

Congratulations!

You have finally worked through this entire text and have mastered some fundamental strategies that will enable you to continue reading authentic material in Spanish. As indicated in the "Note to Students" it is really not such an impossible task. Throughout this course, you have had to apply many reading skills and think critically about the texts presented, from simple to more complex. You can now read with confidence and explore the Hispanic world, raising your level of awareness of other cultures and understanding more through the interpretive techniques that you have been taught.

You have already seen the value in summarizing material, so here is a quick review of the fundamental reading strategies that have guided you through this course.

Pre-reading

Take a quick look at the entire context checking for format features. Use your background knowledge to look for similarities in what you already know. Scan for cognates and be ready to guess as you try to identify the topic. Ask yourself the fundamental questions of **who, what, where, when, why** and **how.** Skim for more exact information and details.

Decoding

Approach the reading passage line by line, paragraph by paragraph. Identify the main ideas by finding the topic sentence and using the last sentence in the paragraph to guide you for further comprehension. For more detailed understanding of key words that are not cognates, use the dictionary skills that you have developed. See how the text is structured, look for the clues that will aid you in understanding such as titles, subtitles, symbols, graphs, pictures and captions. Make some predictions about the topic and ask yourself questions about the content. Be aware of false cognates, idioms and metaphors. Make a summary of your reading and ask yourself more detailed questions about the content for close reading.

Comprehension and Interpretation

Be aware that you will most likely have to re-read the text or passage. Take another look at the organization and context and consider the author's point of view, the tone and the cultural context. Think about what you have read and formulate your own opinion. What response would you give to the author? Take your time and enjoy the reading experience!

¡ADELANTE Y BUENA SUERTE!

CREDITS

Grateful acknowledgement is made for the following:

Susana Aguirre Hernández, Universidad Nacional Autónoma de México – *"¿Qué es una leyenda?", "Día de gran tradición en México", "Días de celebración", "Una comida muy mexicana", "Pastel Azteca"* p. 23, 27, 45

Américas – Magazine published by the Organization of American Status (*Américas es una publicación de la Organización de los Estados Americanos, organismo regional del hemisferio occidental, www.Americas.oas.org*) – for the use of the following articles with permission:

"Contra los delitos cibernéticos", "En lo alto de Caracas", "El nuevo museo del niño" (Octubre, 2003*)* p. 36, 50, 51

"La educación: clave del desarrollo", "Rock y Roll en español", "El centro de gravedad" (Diciembre, 2003*)* p. 37, 59

"En defensa del océano", "La verdadera del dios de los báculos" (Agosto, 2003*)* p. 63

***En español* Discover – Un mundo de ciencia tecnología**
Magazine published by *Ideas and Capital*, Miami, Florida

"Comida de los osos", "Un viaje vital", "Los vikingos", "El universo y la informática", "El origen de los antibióticos" (Agosto, 2003*)* p. 34, 35, 48, 52, 64

MUY INTERESANTE – *(*Magazine published by *Editorial Eres S.A. de C.V. México, D.F. Año XV No. 2)*

"Llegan los supermexicanos" p. 64

Narraciones españolas para estudiantes extranjeros. Juan D. Luque Duran Nivel superior Sociedad General Española de Librería S.A. 1987 Avenida Valdelaparra 29 – 28100 Alcobendas (Madrid) p. 60, 65, 66

Appendix A: Grammar Guidelines

I. Accentuation.

Although correct pronunciation is not essential for this course, knowledge of word stress *is*, for it is linked to the written accent.

- In spoken Spanish any word that ends in a vowel, **-n**, or **–s** is stressed on the 2nd-to-last syllable. The following words fall into this group:

  primo *casa* *mono* *margen* *reglas* *toman*

- If a word ends in any other consonant besides **–n** or **–s**, the last syllable must be stressed.

  ciudad *general* *comer* *cicatriz*

- A written accent is required when the rules above do not apply.

  música *lápiz* *compás* *papá* *césped* *tomó* *dándomelo*

  Written accents can also have a purely grammatical function and are used for the following:

(1) Indicating interrogative and exclamatory words:
¿Dónde? ¿Cómo? ¿Qué? ¿Cuánto? ¿Por qué? ¿Cuándo? ¿Cuál/es? ¿Quién/es?

(2) Distinguishing demonstrative pronouns from demonstrative adjectives, though this rule is no longer absolute:
éste/ésta (“this one”) vs *este/a* (“this”, adj.)
ése/ésa (“that one”) vs *ese/esa* (“that”, adj.)
aquél/aquélla (“that one”) vs. *aquel/aquella* (“that”, adj.)

(3) Distinguishing between two words that are pronounced the same but have different meanings:
el (“the”)/*él* (“he”) *si* (“if”)’ *sí* (“yes”) *solo* (“alone”)/*sólo* (“only”) *de* (“of, from”)/*dé* (first and third-person singular of present subjunctive of *dar)* *aun* (“even”, adverb)/*aún*

(“still”, adverb) *mi* (“my,” possessive adjective)/*mí* (“me,” object of a preposition)

II. **Articles** Words that precede nouns (person, place or thing) in order to limit or give definiteness and are categorized as **definite** or **indefinite.** They denote **gender** (masculine or feminine) and **number** (singular or plural).

- **Definite articles** denote specificity in reference to a group or class.

masculine singular	*el*	**masculine plural**	*los*
feminine singular	*la*	**feminine plural**	*las*

- **Definite articles** have only one form in English **(the)** and are used with the nouns they modify.

la mujer	*la casa*	*las mujeres*	*las casas*
el joven	*el museo*	*los jóvenes*	*los museos*

Note that the **gender** and **number** of the noun is reflected in the use of the definite article.

Indefinite articles denote generality and non-specific references.

masculine singular	*un* (“a/an”)
masculine plural	*unos* (“some,” “a few”)
feminine singular	una (a/an)
feminine plural	*unas* (“some,” “a few”)

un hombre/unos hombres	*una gata/ unas gatas*
un coche/unos coches	*una ventana/unas ventanas*

III. **Nouns** A noun is a person, place or thing. There are **proper nouns** (*México, la Casa Blanca, Mario)* and **common nouns** (*una flor, la playa, una escuela)* belonging to one of two gender classes, masculine or feminine. There

are also categories of nouns that refer to humans and animals and do reflect their gender.
Nouns in Spanish end in a vowel, typically **a, e, o,** or in the consonants **s, n, d, l, r** and sometimes **m** and **z.**

el hombre *la muchacha* *el perro* *la pera*

All other nouns are designated masculine or feminine and refer to grammatical categories.

Most nouns that end in **a** are feminine. Other feminine endings include *–dad /tad, -ción, -sión, -z*

Most nouns that end in **o** are masculine. Other masculine endings include *–or, -e,* and *–ma.* (*programa, sistema, drama, problema*)

Some of these patterns are broken by exceptions that must be learned. A few of these are *el día, la mano, la tarde, el lápiz.*

As a general rule, the plural of a noun ending in a vowel is formed by adding **–s.** The plural of nouns ending in a consonant is formed by adding **–es.**

la ensalada/las ensaladas *el café/los cafés*
la ciudad/las ciudades *el árbol/los árboles*

A noun ending in **z** changes to *–ces* in the plural as in *pez, peces; luz, luces*

IV. **Adjectives** These are words that describe, limit meaning or make the noun or pronoun more definite. They are listed as descriptive, numerical, possessive, demonstrative, quantitative, and indefinite and take the gender of the nouns they modify and agree with in number.
una noche oscura/ unas noches oscuras el libro breve/ los libros breves

- **Placement of adjectives – General Guidelines**

Adjectives in these categories precede the noun they modify.

1. Numerical adjectives: *tres libros, veinte estudiantes*
2. Ordinal adjectives: *la cuarta casa, la décima vez*
3. Descriptive adjectives (emphasis, poetic device): *la blanca nieve*
4. Possessive adjectives (short form) *tu amigo, mis clases*
5. Demonstrative adjectives: *este problema, estos mapas*
6. Quantitative adjectives: *muchos niños, otras ideas*
7. Indefinite adjectives: *ningún profesor, tal cosa*

Adjectives in these categories follow the nouns they modify.

1. Descriptive adjectives: *unas flores bonitas, la casa grande*
2. Possessive adjectives (long form): *una amiga suya, esos papeles tuyos*

V. **Adverbs** These are words that modify verbs, adjectives, and other adverbs. They fall into several different groups:

- **Time** – Answers the question "when"?
  ahora, más tarde, ayer, anoche, por la mañana, etc.
- **Manner** – Answers the question "how"?
  bastante, bien, mal, brevemente, valiosamente, etc.
- **Frequency** – Answers the question "how often"?
  generalmente, siempre, todos los días, a veces, etc.
- **Place** – Answers the question "where"?
  ahí, aquí, debajo de, encima de, etc.
- **Affirmation** - Examples of this type of adverb are:
  sí, claro, por supuesto, sin duda
- **Negation** – Examples of this type of adverb are:
  no, nadie, tampoco, de ninguna manera

Adverbs are also formed by adding *–mente* to the **feminine singular** form of the adjective. This is like adding **–ly** in English. If the adjective has an accent mark, then the adverb retains the accent.

Adjective	**Adverb**
rápido	*rápidamente*
fast	quickly
exacto	*exactamente*
exact	exactly
inmediato	*inmediatamente*
immediate	immediately

If the adjective does not have a feminine form, then *mente* is added to the singular.

feliz	*felizmente*
happy	happily
triste	*tristemente*
sad	sadly

Adverbs are usually placed before adjectives or after the verbs they modify.

Es verdaderamente increíble. It's really incredible!
Comían lentamente. They were eating slowly.

If there are two or more adverbs in a series, the last takes the *–mente* ending.

Leen lenta y cuidadosamente. They read slowly and carefully.

VI. Pronouns A pronoun takes the place of a noun. Spanish pronouns are classified into the following groups.

- **Subject pronouns**

yo	*nosotros/as*
tú	*vosotros/as*

él	*ellos*
ella	*ellas*
usted	*ustedes*

Yo escribo en mi cuaderno.	I write in my notebook.
Ustedes salen temprano.	You people leave early.

Subject pronouns identify who is doing the action and refers to people. Since the verb ending indicates its subject, the use of the subject pronoun is not required but it helps to clarify the 3rd person or to emphasize the subject.

Ella dejó las llaves aquí.	She left the keys here.
Yo no dije eso.	I didn't say that.

- **Reflexive pronouns**

me	*nos*
te	*os*
se	*se*

The reflexive pronouns show that the subject of the sentence does something to himself, herself, themselves. The subject does the action and receives the action.

Ella se levanta temprano.	She gets (herself) up early.
Los niños se bañan.	The children take a bath

(bathe themselves.)

- **Direct object pronouns**

me	*nos*
te	*os*
lo/la	*los/las*

The direct object of a sentence tells who or what is affected directly by the verb. The direct object pronoun replaces this noun in the sentence and is placed directly before the conjugated verb or attached to an infinitive, present participle or a command form.

Leemos muchos libros. Los leemos. We read many books. We read them.
¡Di la verdad! ¡Dila! Tell the truth. Tell it.

Indirect object pronouns

me	*nos*
te	*os*
le	*les*

Indirect objects tell who is affected by the action of a verb: to whom/what or for whom/what the action is done. The indirect object pronoun replaces this noun and is placed before the conjugated verb or is attached to an infinitive, a present participle or command form.
Dime la verdad. Tell me the truth. (Tell the truth to me.)
Nos escriben una carta. They write us a letter. (They write a letter to us.)

It is also possible to have a double object pronoun in the sentence. In this case, the indirect object pronoun always comes before the direct object pronoun.

Hazmelo, por favor. Do it for me, please.
Nos los mandan por correo. They send them to us by mail.

If *le/les* is used with the direct object pronouns *lo, la, los, las,* then *le/les* change to *se.*

Pienso darle mis apuntes.→*Pienso dárselos.*
I'm planning to give him my notes.→I'm planning to give them to him.

- **Prepositional pronouns**

mí	*nosotros/as*
ti	*vosotros/as*
él	*ellos*
ella	*ellas*
usted	*ustedes*

These pronouns are used as objects of a preposition and are the same as the subject pronouns except for 1st and 2nd person. Note the use of *conmigo, contigo.* These are special forms used with the preposition *con.*

Estas flores son para ti. These flowers are for you.
Ella salió con él. She went out with him.

- **Possessive pronouns**

mío/a/os/as	*nuestro/a/os/as*
tuyo/a/os/as	*vuestro/a/os/as*
suyo/a/os/as	*suyo/a/os/as*

Possessive pronouns indicate possession and are usually used with the definite article. This article may be omitted after the verb *ser.*

Estos libros son míos. These books are mine.
Parece que los tuyos desaparecieron. It looks like yours disappeared.

- **Demonstrative pronouns**

éste/a	*ése/a*
estos/as	*ésos/as*
aquél/lla	*aquéllos/as*

Demonstrative pronouns, (i.e. "this one," "that one," "these," "those") replace the nouns to which they refer and show proximity *(éste)* to the speaker or relative distance from the speaker (*ése, aquél*) in space and time.

¿Te gustan éstos o ésos? Do you like these or those?
Prefiero aquéllos. I prefer those over there.

There are also three neuter demonstrative pronouns that refer to unidentified ideas, statements or objects whose gender is unknown. The pronouns are *esto, eso,* and *aquello.*

No entiendo qué quiere decir esto. I don't understand what this means.
Eso sí nos gusta mucho. We really like that.
¿Qué fue todo aquello? What was all that?

- **Relative pronouns**

que, donde, quien/es, el cual , la cual, los cuales, las cuales, el que, la que, los que, las que, lo que, lo cual, cuyo/a, cuyos/as

The relative pronouns connect two clauses and refer to a person or thing in the preceding clause.

Los estudiantes que toman este curso, Español 7, son muy inteligentes.
The students who take Spanish 7 are very intelligent.
Comprendo lo que estás diciendo.
I understand what you are saying.

Mariela plantó unas flores, entre las cuales se hallaban unas rosas.
Mariela planted some flowers; among which a few roses were found.

Estas son las personas a quienes conocimos ayer.
These are the people whom we met yesterday.

VII. Verbs

Spanish verbs fall into three basic categories: **-ar**, **-er**, and **–ir** verbs. The following chart shows all verb tenses for the **–ar** verb *amar* ("to love").

Tense	**1st Person**	**2nd Person**	**3rd Person**	**English equivalent**
Pres. Indicative	*amo*	*amas*	*ama*	"I love, do love"
	amamos	*amáis*	*aman*	
Preterite	*amé*	*amaste*	*amó*	"I loved, did love"
	amamos	*amasteis*	*amaron*	
Imperfect	*amaba*	*amabas*	*amaba*	"I loved, used to love"
	amábamos	*amabais*	*amaban*	
Future	*amaré*	*amarás*	*amará*	"I will love"
	amaremos	*amaréis*	*amarán*	
Conditional	*amaría*	*amarías*	*amaría*	"I would love"
	amaríamos	*amaríais*	*amarían*	
Pres. subjunctive	*ame* *amemos*	*ames* *améis*	*ame* *amen*	"I love, do love"
Past Subjunctive	*amara*	*amaras*	*amara*	"I loved, did love"
	amáramos	*amarais*	*amaran*	
Pres. Perfect indicative	*he amado*	*has amado*	*ha amado*	"I have loved"
	hemos amado	*habéis amado*	*han amado*	
Pluperfect indicative	*había amado*	*habías amado*	*había amado*	"I had loved"

Tense	**1st Person**	**2nd Person**	**3rd Person**	**English equivalent**
Pluperfect Indicative (con’t)	*habíamos amado*	*habíais amado*	*habían amado*	
Future perfect	*habré amado*	*habrás amado*	*habrá amado*	“I will have loved”
	habremos amado	*habréis amado*	*habrán amado*	
Conditional perfect	*habría amado*	*habrías amado*	*habría amado*	“I would have loved”
	habríamos amado	*habría amado*	*habrían amado*	
Present perfect subjunctive	*haya amado*	*hayas amado*	*haya amado*	“I have loved”
	hayamos amado	*hayáis amado*	*hayan amado*	
Pluperfect subjunctive	*hubiera amado*	*hubieras amado*	*hubiera amado*	“I had loved”
	hubiéramos amado	*hubierais amado*	*hubieran amado*	
Imperative	-	*ama*	*ame*	(Command forms)
	amemos	*amad*	*amen*	

The following chart shows the tenses for the regular **–ir** verb *vivir* ("to live").

Tense	**1st Person**	**2nd Person**	**3rd person**	**English equivalent**
Pres. Indicative	*vivo*	*vives*	*vive*	"I live, do live"
	vivimos	*vivís*	*viven*	
Preterite	*viví*	*viviste*	*vivió*	"I lived, did live"
	vivimos	*vivisteis*	*vivieron*	
Imperfect	*vivía*	*vivías*	*vivía*	"I lived, used to live"
	vivíamos	*vivíais*	*vivían*	
Future	*viviré*	*vivirás*	*vivirá*	"I will live"
	viviremos	*viviréis*	*vivirán*	
Conditional	*viviría*	*vivirías*	*viviría*	"I would live"
	viviríamos	*viviríais*	*vivirían*	
Pres.subjunctive	*viva*	*vivas*	*viva*	"I live, do live"
	vivamos	*viváis*	*vivan*	
Past subjunctive	*viviera*	*vivieras*	*viviera*	"I lived, did live"
	viviéramos	*vivierais*	*vivieran*	
Pres. Perfect indicative	*he vivido*	*has vivido*	*ha vivido*	"I have lived"
	hemos vivido	*habéis vivido*	*han vivido*	

Pluperfect indicative	*había vivido*	*habías vivido*	*había vivido*	"I had lived"
	habíamos vivido	*habíais vivido*	*habían vivido*	
Future perfect	*habré vivido*	*habrás vivido*	*habrá vivido*	"I will have lived"
	habremos vivido	*habréis vivido*	*habrán vivido*	
Conditional perfect	*habría vivido*	*habrías vivido*	*habría vivido*	"I would have lived"
	habríamos vivido	*habrías vivido*	*habrían vivido*	
Present perfect subjunctive	*haya vivido*	*hayas vivido*	*haya vivido*	"I have lived"
	hayamos vivido	*hayáis vivido*	*hayan vivido*	
Pluperfect subjunctive	*hubiera vivido*	*hubieras vivido*	*hubiera vivido*	"I had lived"
	hubiéramos vivido	*hubierais vivido*	*hubieran vivido*	
Imperative	-	*vive*	*viva*	(Command forms)
	vivamos	*vivid*	*vivan*	

- Many verbs have an irregular first-person singular in the present tense:

hago (*hacer*), *doy* (*dar*), *traigo* (*traer*), *oigo* (*oír*), *valgo* (*valer*), *conozco* (*conocer*), *produzco* (*producir*), *veo* (*ver*), *sé* (*saber*), *pongo* (*poner*), *salgo* (*salir*)

Verbs ending in **–cer** or **–cir** add a **z** before the final **c** of the stem:

conozco (*conocer*), *produzco* (*producir*).

Verbs ending in **–ger** and **–gir** replace the **g** of the stem with **j**:

escojo (*escoger*), *corrijo* (*corregir*)

Verbs ending in **–guir** drop the **u:**

sigo (seguir), consigo (conseguir)

Verbs ending in **–uir** (*destruir, construir, disminuir*) require a **y** in all but the first-person plural and second-person plural forms:

destruyo, destruyes, destruye, destruimos, destruís, destruyen

And finally, a relatively small group of verbs ending in **–iar** and **–uar** must carry a written accent over **i** and **u** in all but the first-person plural and second person-plural forms to indicate a that the vowel is pronounced fully and not as a diphthong.

enviar: *envío, envías, envías, enviamos, enviáis, envían*

actuar: *actúo, actúas, actúa, actuamos, actuáis, actúan*

- The present tense also includes many **stem-changing verbs** in which all singular and third-person plural forms undergo a vocalic change in the thematic vowel.

  (e→ie) *querer, pensar, cerrar, entender*

  Ex: *qu**ie**ro, qu**ie**res, qu**ie**re, queremos, queréis, qu**ie**ren*

  (e→i) *seguir, pedir, servir, repetir*

  Ex: ***si**go, **si**gues, **si**gue, seguimos, seguís, **si**guen*
  (o→ue) *contar, almorzar, dormir, morir*
  Ex: *c**ue**nto, c**ue**ntas, c**ue**nta, contamos, contáis, c**ue**ntan*

  (u→ue) *jugar*

  Ex: *j**ue**go, j**ue**gas, j**ue**ga, jugamos, jugáis, j**ue**gan*

- The only difference between **–er** and **–ir** verbs is found in the present tense endings.
- The **preterite** and **imperfect** are both past tenses and reflect different aspectual distinctions. The preterite is used for events viewed by the speaker as having been completed.

A great number of verbs have irregular preterite stems that take the following endings: **-e**, **-iste**, **-o**, **-imos**, **-isteis**, **-ieron**. Such verbs include *andar* (*anduv-*), *estar* (*estuv-*), *tener* (*tuv-*), *caber* (*cup-*), *haber* (*hub-*), *poder* (*pud-*), *poner* (*pus-*), *saber* (*sup-*), *querer* (*quis-*), *venir* (*vin-*)

A smaller group of verbs—*decir* (*dij-*), *traer* (*tra-*), *conducer* (*conduj-*), *producir* (*produj-*)—drop the **i** of the third-person plural ending and replace it with **j** (*dijeron/trajeron/condujeron/produjeron*)

Ser and *ir* share the same forms in the preterite tense: *fui, fuiste, fue, fuimos fuisteis, fueron.*

Stem-changing **–ar** and **–er** verbs of the present tense do not show the same patterns in the preterite, whereas stem-changing **–ir** verbs such as *dormir* (o→ue→u) or *pedir* (e→i→i) are altered in the third-person forms only: ***durmió/durmieron, pidió/pidieron.***

Verbs ending in **–car**, **-gar**, and **–zar** require a spelling change in the first-person singular of the preterite (**c→qu**, **g→gu**, **z→c**): *bus**qué**, lle**gué**, empecé*

The imperfect tense is used for past habitual actions or events viewed by the speaker as ongoing in the past. Only three verbs are irregular in the imperfect:

ser: *era, eras, era, éramos, erais, eran.*
ir: *iba, ibas, iba, íbamos, ibais, iban*
ver: *veía, veías, veía, veíamos, veíais, veían*

- There are four **subjunctive tenses** in Spanish (present/past/present perfect/pluperfect) and each can be translated roughly as its indicative counterpart. In other words, *he amado* and *haya amado* both mean "I have loved", *vivió* and *viviera* mean "he/she/you lived", and *habíamos aprendido* and *hubiéramos aprendido* equate to "we had learned." Alternate sets of endings in **-se** exist for the past subjunctive and pluperfect subjunctive tenses: *amase, amases, amases*, etc., *aprendiese, aprendieses, aprendiese*, etc., *hubiese amado, hubieses amado, hubiese amado*, etc., *hubiese aprendido, hubieses aprendido, hubiese aprendido*, etc.

- The perfect tenses consist of a form of the auxiliary *haber* and the **past participle**. For most verbs the past participle is formed by adding **–ado** (**-ar** verbs) or **–ido** (**-er/-ir** verbs) to the stem:

am<u>ado</u> aprend<u>ido</u> viv<u>ido</u>

If the verb stem of an **–er** or **–ir** verb ends in *-a, -e,* or *-o*, an accent is needed over the **i**: *caído, poseído, oído.*

Many verbs in Spanish, however, such as those in parentheses below, have irregular past participles which must be memorized:

abierto (abrir), cubierto (cubrir), descubierto (descubrir), descrito (describir), devuelto (devolver), dicho (decir), escrito (escribir), hecho (hacer), impreso (imprimir), muerto (morir), puesto (poner), roto (romper), vuelto (volver), visto (ver)

- *Ser* and *estar* both mean "to be" but are used in different contexts. *Ser* typically is used for:

1) Intrinsic personality or physical characteristics.

Mis padres ***son*** *muy estrictos. Elena* ***es*** *rubia.*

2) Identifying people, places, days, dates or things.

Ese señor ***es*** *mi tío. Sacramento* ***es*** *una ciudad bonita.*
Hoy ***es*** *lunes. Mañana* ***es*** *el 23 de julio. Esto* ***es*** *un armario.*

3) Expressing nationality or profession.

Mis abuelos ***eran*** *italianos. Miguel* ***es*** *ingeniero.*

4) Indicating place of origin (after *de*).

Juan Carlos ***es*** *de Chile.*

5) Showing possession (also after *de*).

Ese coche ***es*** *de mi amiga Ana.*

6) Telling time.

¿Qué hora ***es****?* ***Son*** *las dos.*

7) Explaining what something is made from.

Mi camisa ***es*** *de algodón.*

8) Discussing when and where an event occurs.

La fiesta ***será*** *a las dos en el apartamento de Mario.*

9) In passive constructions, usually with an expressed agent introduced by *por*.

Todas las ventanas ***fueron*** *cerradas por el profesor.*

10) Expressing a generalization or commonly-held opinion or idea.

Es *importante/interesante/ridículo/bueno/malo...(que)...*

Estar has fewer overall uses. It can be used for:

1) Stating the physical location of someone or something in space or time.

Mis hermanos ***están*** *en México ahora. El banco* ***está*** *al lado del mercado.*
Ya ***estamos*** *en febrero.*

2) Indicating physical or emotional states at a given point in time or conditions that result from a previous action.

***Estoy** muy triste hoy.* *Jorge y Marco **estaban** cansados después de correr 5 millas.*
*La puerta **está** cerrada.* (i.e., as a result of someone closing it)

3) Expressing conditions which deviate from the norm expected by the speaker.

*¡Qué alto **está** Joselito!* (i.e., I didn't expect him to be so tall, but he's grown!)

4) The **progressive tenses**, which emphasize the ongoing nature of the action.

***Estamos** caminando hacia el parque.*
("We are walking towards the park", i.e., right now)

*Juan **estaba** cruzando la calle cuando lo vieron sus amigos.*
("Juan was crossing the street when his friends saw him")

While in theory the verb *estar* can be employed in any tense in these constructions, typically it is used in either the present or imperfect. The **present participle** required in all the progressive tenses (ending in *–ando* for **–ar** verbs and *–iendo* for **–er** and **–ir** verbs) is formed from the stem of the infinitive: *cantando, bebiendo, escribiendo*. Stem-changing **–ir** verbs such as *dormir, pedir, seguir* and *preferir*, which undergo a stem change in the third-person singular and plural forms of the preterite, transfer the same change to the present participle: *durmiendo, pidiendo, siguiendo, prefiriendo*. Certain **–er** and **-ir** verbs such as *leer, traer, caer, oír* and *ir* require the addition of **y** in the present participle: *leyendo, trayendo, cayendo, oyendo,* and *yendo.*

- The imperative is used to express direct commands in Spanish. All negative commands, as well as affirmative commands for *Ud.* and *Uds.*, coincide formally with the present subjunctive tense: (Negative) *¡No compres!* (*tú*), *¡No compre!* (Ud.), *¡No compremos!* (*nosotros/as*), *¡No compréis!* (*vosotros/as*), *¡No compren!* (*Uds.*). (Affirmative) *¡Compre!* (*Ud.*), *¡Compren!* (*Uds.*).

The affirmative form of all *tú* commands is the third-person singular of the present indicative tense: *¡Compra! ¡Aprende! ¡Vive!*.

The following forms, however, are the irregular *tú* commands:

ten (*tener*), *ven* (*venir*), *pon* (*poner*), *sal* (*salir*), *ve* (*ir*), *sé* (*ser*), *haz* (*hacer*), *di* (*decir*)

For *vosotros/as*, drop the **r** from the infinitive and add **d**: *¡Comprad! ¡Aprended! ¡Vivid!*. If the verb is reflexive, drop the **d** and add the ending **–os** to the verb stem, noting that reflexive verbs ending in **–ir** require a written accent: *¡Acostaos! ¡Poneos! ¡Dormíos!* One verb—*irse*—maintains the **d** in the affirmative vosotros command form: *¡Idos!*

Appendix B: Using the Bilingual Dictionary.

I. What makes a good dictionary?

Finding a good bilingual dictionary can be a daunting task and certain factors such as price or convenience often weigh more heavily than inherent value. For this class, it is absolutely essential that you have at your disposal at all times the best possible dictionary that you can find. Typically, dictionaries come in two types: paperback and hardbound. Paperback dictionaries are to be used for convenience and by their very nature usually contain fewer entries and overall information about the language in question. Hardbound dictionaries, on the other hand, are much larger and informative but not as easy to carry around. Ideally, you should have one of each available to you and should consider the following questions when contemplating which dictionary to buy or use:

- First of all, when was the dictionary last *edited* as opposed to *printed*? In other words, when was it last revised? If your dictionary was re-printed two years ago but has not been re-edited since 1968, you are bound to come across some major problems. Look up such recent terminology as *Internet* or *e-mail* to see how up-to-date the dictionary is.
- How many words and expressions does it contain? It should have at least 30,000 words, but the more, the merrier! You do not want to be constantly disappointed by a dictionary that lacks important vocabulary.
- How much information is given for each entry? Is there just a one-word translation or is there detailed grammatical information with example sentences and idiomatic and or dialectical usage? Are multiple definitions given? If only one line is used for each entry, your dictionary will be of little help to you.
- Does the dictionary contain separate grammatical indexes (verb charts, common suffix lists, specialized vocabulary lists such as country names or currencies, etc.)? Any dictionary worth its weight does, but you should check just in case so as to avoid having to purchase further materials.

Activity A: Examine your dictionary and write a detailed summary of its sections in the exact order in which they appear.

II. Deciphering dictionary entries.

You should have little trouble finding entries for Spanish words in your dictionary, although a certain amount of care is required with the letters **ch**, **ll**, **ñ**, and **rr,** which do not exist in English and each of which actually represents only one sound. Until recently, words beginning in **ch**, **ll**, and **ñ**—there are no words that begin with **rr**—were given separately in different groupings following **c**, **l**, and **n**, respectively. (Older dictionaries may still reflect this practice.) Now, however, words such as **churro** and **llorar** are included under **c** and **l** (after, say, **cetro** but before **cicatriz** in the case of the former and after **liviano** but before **lobo** for the latter). In word-internal position, **ch**, **ll,** and **ñ** are alphabetized in the same way. The letter **ñ** retains its status as having a separate list of words that begin with it, though relatively few words in Spanish do. The letter **rr** denotes the "trilled r" characteristic of Spanish and only occurs in word-internal position (**carro**, **perro**, **guitarra**). The letter **r** is alphabetized before **rr** and so a word like **carpintero** will appear immediately before **carraca.**

Activity B. Look up the following words and place them in the correct alphabetical order.

1. *cojo, churro, cena, chorro, chocolate, chincheta, calavera, culebra*:____
   ____
2. *llegar, legar, lente, llave, lloriquear, luz, liceo, ladrar*:____
   ____
3. *cachetada, cacatúa, cachorro, cachimbo, cadera, caballo, café, cachondeo*:___________________________________
   ____
4. *polo, pellejo, pollo, pillar, pilar, palo, picar, pulir, polio, pelo*:____
   ____

Once you find the word you are looking for, however, the real work begins. Consider the following entry from the Oxford Spanish-English dictionary for the word **pena**.

> **pena** *f* **1 (a)** (tristeza): **tenía/sentía mucha ~** he was *o* felt very sad; **me da ~ verlo** it upsets me *o* it makes me sad to see it; **a mí la que me da ~ es su mujer** its his wife I feel sorry for; **está que da ~** she's in a terrible state; **me da ~ tener que decírselo** it hurts me to have to tell him; **lloraba con tanta ~** he was crying so bitterly **(b)** (lástima) pity, shame; **¡qué ~!** What a pity *o* shame!; **es una ~ que**...it's a pity (that)..., ***de ~*** (Esp) terrible; ***estar hecho una ~*** to be in a sorry *o* terrible state; ***sin ~ ni gloria*** almost unnoticed; ***vale or merece la ~*** it's worth it; **vale la ~ leerlo/visitarlo** it's worth reading/a visit; **no vale la ~ intentar convencerlo** there's no point *o* it's not worth trying to persuade him
>
> **2 penas** *fpl* **(a)** (problemas) sorrows (*pl*); **ahogar las ~s** to drown one's sorrows; **me contó sus ~s** he told me his troubles *o* (literal *or* humorous) woes; ***a duras ~s*** (apenas) hardly; (con dificultad) with difficulty **(b)** (penalidades) hardship; **pasamos muchas ~s** we suffered great hardship **bajo** *or* **so ~ de** (formal) on pain of (formal); **so ~ de repetirme**
>
> **3** (Der) sentence; **la ~ maxima** the maximum sentence; at the risk of repeating myself **pena capital** *or* **de muerte** death penalty
>
> **4** (AmL exc CS) (vergüenza) embarrassment; **¡qué ~!** How embarrassing!; **me da mucha ~ pedírselo** I'm too embarrassed to ask him; ***quitado de la ~*** (Méx) blithely, gaily
>
> **5** (Per) (fantasma) ghost

This detailed entry at first glance appears rather complicated, but in reality is very organized, easy to understand and informative. Indeed, it tells us much about the word in question thanks to its numerous format cues and abbreviations. First of all, it clearly shows us through thc usc of numbcrs that **pena** has fivc basic meanings and it gives the most common first. It also includes Spanish equivalents in parentheses, sub-meanings (for example, **1a** and **1b**), clear example sentences and idiomatic usage (in boldface and italics), as well as dialectical information (Esp=Spain, AmL=Latin America, CS=Cono Sur, Méx=Mexico, Per=Peru).

To better understand such entries, it's a good idea to learn your dictionary's abbreviations as soon as possible. Among the more common Spanish abbreviations that denote grammatical information are:
F=feminine noun (person, place, or thing)
M=masculine noun (person place or thing)
S=singular
Pl=plural
Adj=adjective (word which describes a noun)
V.t.=transitive verb (verb usually requiring a direct object)
V.intr.=intransitive verb (verb which can stand on its own)
V.ref.=reflexive verb (verb which must be conjugated in Spanish with the pronouns **me, te, se, nos, os, se**)
Adv=adverb (word which describes the manner, place, or time of an action)
Art=article (word which points out the noun)

Other abbreviations may refer to countries, geographical regions, or vocabulary groups.

It is incumbent upon you to consult your own dictionaries and memorize the more common abbreviations.

Activity C: In pairs, look up the following words, write down the complete dictionary entry and share your findings with other groups.

1. *soplar* 2. *lentitud* 3. *acordar* 4. *este* 5. *bien* 6. *venir*

Appendix C: Current Web Addresses to the Hispanic World

The following web addresses have been included so that you may have a ready reference as you search for additional authentic materials in Spanish. The links to these addresses sometimes change but a final check revealed that these are still good.

- www.yahoo.com
- www.google.com

Look for links for newspapers, magazines and cultural materials. The following are more specific sites that will enable you to search by country and find more information on people and places.

- www.spanish.mhhe.com (This is the *¿Qué tal?* site from McGraw-Hill Companies)
- www.latino.com
- www.nicaragua-online.com
- www.usac.edu.gt
- www.escapeartist.com/honduras/honduras.htm
- www.domrep.org
- www.latinworld.com/countries/bolivia
- www.ecuador.org/ecuador
- www.chile-online.com
- www.latinworld.com/countries/paraguay
- www.tourspain.es/

There are many more sites that you can discover on your own. The following is a link to the Spanish 7 webpage developed specifically for this course by Professor Mariela Santana-Howard and Magaly Lagunas-Carvacho, which will give you some extra reading practice: www.csus.edu/indiv/s/santana

¡Buen viaje!

Appendix D: Guide for a Web Project.

An integral part of any Spanish reading proficiency class should entail the exploration of Hispanic cultures by way of current events. The best, quickest, and most effective way to do this nowadays is via the Internet using a search engine such as Google or Yahoo. (For Google, go to www.google.com, click *Directory*, then click *Español* at the bottom of the page, then click *Países*. For Yahoo, go to www.yahoo.com and scroll down for any Spanish-speaking countries.)

As you look for news articles or stories that pique your interest, try to stay positive and focus on things that are of true cultural relevance. In other words, avoid stories that merely summarize natural disasters, accidents, a specific crime that took place, etc., and focus on people, places, or events that have some sort of cultural meaning and importance, at least in your opinion. Avoid articles that are not about the country you are researching (such as those which merely detail international news) or are merely a collection of boring, useless data (e.g., the latest Gross National Product figures). Look for lengthy, substantial prose articles which go beyond two or three paragraphs. Don't worry if you cannot immediately find a good article—this search is an important part of the reading process which will help you refine your overall comprehension skills.

Once you have located and printed an article that you find interesting, read it several times using the strategies you have studied in order to get the gist of the story or news event discussed. Eventually, you should underline all vocabulary that you do not understand and make a bilingual word list consisting of the following: (1) the word in Spanish, (2) its part of speech (noun, adjective, verb, adverb, etc.), and (3) its English equivalent. For all verb forms, give the infinitive and verb tense.

After completing your word list, write a brief summary about the story itself. Detail the "who," "what," "why," "where" and "how" of the story, but don't give a line-by-line translation—just a summary is needed. In your summary point out to your instructor any problematic passages or vocabulary that you may have encountered. Finally, be prepared to discuss your article in class. Why did you find it interesting? And what does it tell you about the culture in question?